To Susan Riskin

THE SEA HORSE

Play by Edward J. Moore; staged by Marshall W. Mason; setting by David Potts; lighting by Cheryl Thacker; costumes by Jennifer von Mayrhauser; presented by Kermit Bloomgarden, Max Allentuck and Orin Lehman at The Westside Theatre, April 15, 1974.

Winner of the Vernon Rice Drama Desk Award for outstanding new playwright.

THE CAST

GERTRUDE BLUM ....*Conchata Ferrell*

HARRY BALES .... *Edward J. Moore*

SYNOPSIS

ACT ONE

After closing.

ACT TWO

Following morning.

The Sea Horse

A NEW PLAY

by Edward J. Moore

SAMUEL FRENCH, INC.

25 West 45th Street   NEW YORK 10036
7623 Sunset Boulevard   HOLLYWOOD 90046
LONDON   *TORONTO*

The Sea Horse

ACT ONE

The Sea Horse is a bar in a California seaport, a dimly-lit, musty, drafty, dreary, unpleasant place. It is about 2:30 A.M., the sound of thunder and a heavy rain can be heard. The bar is empty, it is after closing. As lights come up, we see chairs stacked on the three tables. Two, which are stage right along the wall, the third having been pulled upstage center to clear for mopping. A portable stove has also been moved out of the way, stage right. From the back room upstage right, a loud clatter of bottles is heard as they are accidentally knocked over.

GERTRUDE. (*Offstage. Furious.*) Oh shit!! (*A moment, then,* GERTRUDE BLUM *enters from the back room. She is in her late thirties, a big woman about two hundred pounds, fat, but firm, not flabby, and stands five foot seven or eight.* GERTRUDE *has a strong, sensitive face that hasn't been distorted by her bulk. Her hair is pulled back in a ponytail, she is wearing dark green men's work pants, a long sleeved grey work shirt and black shoes. Her clothes are grubby and she looks tired, work-weary after a long day. Carrying a mop and pail she crosses stage left, sets the pail down, leans the mop against the bar, she stacks several bar stools, moves them out of her way. As she begins to mop, we see* HARRY BALES *running up to the front door, his sea bag over his shoulder, he is dripping wet from the rain. He tries the door, it's locked, knocks.*)

HARRY. Gertrude?! . . . You there?! . . . It's me!! . . . It's Harry, I'm back!! . . . (*Pounding hard.*) Hurry up, will ya! It's pouring like hell out here! I'm

5

getting soaked!! (GERTRUDE *continues mopping, going about her work as if she doesn't hear him.* HARRY *has backed away from the door a few feet and is calling upstairs.*) Gertrude?! You upstairs?!! . . . It's Harry!! I'm back!! . . . Get down here, will ya! My sea bag's getting soaked . . . I'm sopping wet!!! (*A moment, then in disgust crosses back to the door, he hears* GERTRUDE *as she shoves one of the stools out of her way.*) Gertrude, is that you?! Open up, will ya, it's me, it's Harry . . . I'm dripping wet! (*No answer. Getting upset now.*) What the hell's going on?!! (*Pounds very hard on the door.*) Come on!! Let's go!!! Come on!!! Come on!!!! Come on!!!!

GERTRUDE. (*Infuriated at his heavy pounding, shouts.*) ALL RIGHT!!!

HARRY. (*Angrily.*) WELL LET'S GO!!!! (*Mop in hand,* GERTRUDE *crosses to the door, unlatches it.* HARRY *enters.*) What the hell's the matter with you!! (GERTRUDE *goes immediately back to her work, mopping stage right area.* HARRY *closes the door, crosses upstage right, puts his sea bag down next to the coat rack.*) I was yelling my head off out there, couldn't ya hear me!?! (*He takes off his cap, hangs it up, unzips his jacket. Then he turns back, looks at her.*)

GERTRUDE. (*A long pause as she continues to mop, finally she glares at him.*) Yeah, I heard ya!

HARRY. (*Crosses stage left wringing out the bottom of his sweat shirt on the floor.*) Well what took ya so long!? Look at me, I'm drippin' wet!

GERTRUDE. Yeah!

HARRY. (*Behind the bar now, he takes a towel, starts drying his hair.*) Where were ya!?

GERTRUDE. (*Mopping the water he slopped on the floor.*) I was in the back!

HARRY. You don't mean *on* your back do ya . . . who ya got upstairs . . . (*Moves upstage right to stairwell, shouts.*) ANYONE I KNOW!?!

GERTRUDE. Don't go up there!

HARRY. (*Starts crossing toward her, not wanting to fight.*) Oh, givin' 'em a chance to get out huh?! (*Her back to him, he cracks her bottom with the towel, laughs.*) . . . is that it?!

GERTRUDE. (*Turns, looks at him furious.*) What's it to you?!?

HARRY. Nothing! (*Dismisses the possibility of someone really being upstairs.*) . . . it would be a lousy welcome home, though, wouldn't it?

GERTRUDE. What did you expect?!

HARRY. (*Laughs.*) Not that! (GERTRUDE *crosses, takes chairs off downstage right table.*) Come on, don't I get a big hug . . . (*As she crosses carrying the stove he puts his arms around her waist.*) it's me, you forget or something?

GERTRUDE. (*She shoves him away.*) Cut it out!!

HARRY. (*Crossing upstage right.*) This is a damn nice way to treat me!

GERTRUDE. (*She puts the stove downstage, right of center. Continues mopping.*) You're lucky I let you in!

HARRY. Why?!? (*She doesn't answer. A moment, then gesturing upstairs.*) Hey! . . . you really got someone up there!? (*Terribly upset, he moves out of her way as she mops near him. Crosses to upstage center table.*) What the hell did I come back here for?! (*Beginning to shiver.*)

GERTRUDE. Don't ask me!

HARRY. Okay now, what's going on?!

GERTRUDE. I *could* ask you that! (*Takes chairs off upstage right table.*)

HARRY. What?!

GERTRUDE. Sister Katingo! She tied up at pier four at six o'clock this morning! (*Finished mopping, she crosses, goes behind bar stage left. Starts cleaning it off.*)

HARRY. Sister Katingo? . . . that's what's eating you! You don't have anyone upstairs . . . do ya?! (*Laughing, crossing to her.*) you wanted to give me a good shot of pneumonia 'cause I didn't come in right away . . .

(*Goes behind bar, exaggerates his shivering.*) well, look at me . . . I got it! (*She crosses front of bar and as she starts to unstack the stools,* HARRY *puts his arms around her waist. Furious she shakes him off.*)

GERTRUDE. You bastard!!!

HARRY. (*Moves back behind bar.*) Hey . . . wait a minute . . . I stayed aboard the ship!

GERTRUDE. (*Putting stools back in place.*) Of all the crap!!

HARRY. I did, I had to secure!

GERTRUDE. And that took all day!!

HARRY. No . . . I was thinking!

GERTRUDE. (*Stools in place.*) Thinking! (*Crosses, picks up pail and mop.*) You were thinking!! You're gone almost two months and you sit in dock thinking!! (*Turning to him.*) Since when do you think?! . . . You want to stay here, you show me *respect!* (*Mop and pail in hand, exits through curtain to back room.*)

HARRY. (*Crosses after her.*) The crew tell ya I was in on the Sister? . . . (*Stops at doorway.*) Okay, fine! . . . They tell ya they seen me on the pier? . . . In town? . . . No, they didn't! . . . 'Cause I stayed aboard! (*A moment, then:*) Gertrude??

GERTRUDE. (*Offstage.*) Warm up the coffee!!

HARRY. Yeah . . . (*Calls to her as he goes behind the bar.*) Light the stove, will ya? It's freezing in here! (HARRY BALES *is about six foot and weighs around one ninety. He is almost athletic in appearance. He is an intelligent, compassionate man in his late thirties. He is wearing a light weight blue jacket, dark green sweat shirt, tan gabardine pants, logger's low top lace boots and came in wearing an Army jeep cap. He lights the gas under the coffee, takes a whisky bottle and water glass off the back shelf, pours himself a shot, downs it.* GERTRUDE *enters, stands in the doorway, holding a blanket.* HARRY *pours himself another shot.*)

GERTRUDE. You had to take my good stuff . . . (*He

downs the shot.) well, don't gulp it all! Now come on, get that wet coat off!!

HARRY. (*Sets bottle down, crosses to coat rack, unzips his jacket, hangs it up.*) Boy, I got the damn chills now!

GERTRUDE. What about your boots?

HARRY. They're okay.

GERTRUDE. (*Indicating his sweat shirt.*) This too, take it off! (*He does, hangs it up. She touches his pants.*) And your pants are all wet!

HARRY. I ain't changing 'em now, they're at the bottom of my sea bag! (*He is bare-chested.*)

GERTRUDE. (*She puts the blanket around him.*) What happened to your slicker?

HARRY. It's upstairs with the rest of my gear.

GERTRUDE. (*Sarcastically, as she crosses to upstage center table.*) Good place for it!

HARRY. I know, I forgot to take it this trip . . . been like this long?

GERTRUDE. (*Pulling the table back to its place, downstage center.*) Almost a week now.

HARRY. (*He goes behind the bar, picks up the bottle and glass.*) Oh yeah . . . Good for ducks! (*Laughs. With bottle and glass in hand, crosses to window upstage right, looks out.*)

GERTRUDE. (*Having put the chairs under the table, she has crossed behind bar and is now taking cash out of register.*) You really stay aboard?

HARRY. I swear!

GERTRUDE. (*With cash, canvas bag, ledger and pencil she crosses to downstage center table, sits.*) You wasn't with one of your broads?

HARRY. (*Sincerely.*) Hell, no! . . . You know I always come in as soon as I leave the ship!

GERTRUDE. That's all I want! Respect! . . . I don't give a damn what you do after! . . . Your buddies were coming in all day long asking for you . . .

HARRY. Oh, yeah?

GERTRUDE. (*Counting receipts, logs them in the book.*) Yeah! . . . What was I supposed to tell 'em, I didn't even know you was in!? . . . That's a hell of a way to treat me!

HARRY. (*A moment, then crossing to her.*) I didn't want all the guys gaping at me! . . . so I waited for you to close up!

GERTRUDE. Why?!

HARRY. Because I brought ya something private! . . . and then you drowned me out there . . . you know I could get sick! (*He sits. Puts bottle and glass down.*)

GERTRUDE. What did you bring me? (*A moment, then he grins.*) Awwwww . . . it's a present! Ya brought me a present!

HARRY. Yeah?! . . . Well I don't know if I'm gonna give it to ya now!

GERTRUDE. Is it in your bag?

HARRY. . . . I ain't saying.

GERTRUDE. I'll just bring your bag over.

HARRY. (*As she gets up, he puts his arms around her waist, stopping her, he laughs.*) Nooooo . . . not yet . . .

GERTRUDE. I want my present!

HARRY. Okay, okay, you'll get it! . . . But I gotta tell ya something first, it's important . . . now, come on, sit down . . . (*He lets her go, and as he pulls her chair next to him,* GERTRUDE *runs to the sea bag.* HARRY *leaps from his chair, goes after her, grabs hold of the sea bag.*) not now! Wait a minute!

GERTRUDE. I want my present!

HARRY. (*He pulls the bag out of her hands, sits on it. Laughing.*) It's not in there! . . . I left it aboard the ship! . . . Ya see, I didn't want it getting wet! . . . I'll get it for ya tomorrow. (GERTRUDE *crosses back to table, continues counting receipts.* HARRY *gets up, takes sea bag back near coat rack.*) It'll surprise ya tomorrow . . . (*She ignores him.*) Don't ya want to be surprised? (*Enticingly as he crosses, moves up behind her.*) Ohhh . . . it'll surprise ya all right!

GERTRUDE. (*Dryly.*) Did you get that robe I wanted?

HARRY. (*Smiles.*) I tell ya what, I'll give it to ya tomorrow! (*He kisses her on the nose.*)

GERTRUDE. (*A beat, then, with sexual connotations.*) I tell you what, you better give it to me tonight! (*She gets up, they start to kiss passionately, but she pushes him away.*) You're all wet!

HARRY. I wonder why? (*She pokes him, laughs, sits down again. Continues with receipts.* HARRY *leans over her shoulder.*) Busy day huh?

GERTRUDE. Yeah, I was real crowded, can't understand why anyone would want to go out in this weather!

HARRY. That's easy . . . They like ya! (*Goes behind bar, stage left, looks under counter for a snack.*)

GERTRUDE. You mean the booze.

HARRY. (*Taking a box of raisins he sits on bar stool.*) Naw, come on . . . no one around here does business like you!

GERTRUDE. I don't know about anyone else.

HARRY. Well, I'm telling ya . . . they like ya!

GERTRUDE. (*Finished counting receipts, puts money in canvas bag.*) That's good. (*Crosses, takes everything behind bar, puts ledger and cash bag under back counter.*) This run was a lot longer, wasn't it?

HARRY. (*Munching raisins.*) Yeah.

GERTRUDE. What happened?

HARRY. We had to dry-dock in Subic, we had a twisted screw, and a load of frozen fish in number three hold. I'm telling ya it was a mess, we all had to turn to and clean it up. (*A moment, then, with growing excitement.*) Did you know Hank was selling out? I heard the guys talking about it aboard ship . . .

GERTRUDE. Yeah, I know. (*Having taken a tin of cookies from under the counter, she puts some in a bowl.*)

HARRY. (*Gets up, anxious.*) Oh, did he tell ya!? (*Leans on bar.*)

GERTRUDE. (*Returns cooky tin.*) He's had a notice up for months, didn't ya see it?

HARRY. No I didn't! (*Crossing to bulletin board upstage right.*)

GERTRUDE. I'm sick of looking at it!

HARRY. (*Finds the notice, partially hidden under several others, takes it down.*) Oh, yeah . . . (*Worried.*) he couldn't sell it, though, could he?

GERTRUDE. (*Sets coffee cups on bar.*) He was asking too much, I'm sure he'll come down now. (*Quizzically.*) Why?

HARRY. (*Reading.*) I'm thinking of taking it over.

GERTRUDE. (*Exasperated. Pouring the coffee.*) Oh, for Christ's sake, you don't want that shrimper! He hasn't made a decent buck for years!

HARRY. That doesn't matter . . . (*Crosses back to her.*) see, I figure I can turn it into a fishing rental, with guys paying me to take 'em out. You know that's going real big now . . . (*Sits on bar stool.*)

GERTRUDE. Leave it alone!

HARRY. No, I got it all worked out, I bet I could pick it up for three grand. I'm great with engines . . . and it's really not in that bad a shape!

GERTRUDE. It's a wreck!

HARRY. (*Laughs.*) It doesn't matter, it'll be cheap!

GERTRUDE. You don't know what you're getting into!

HARRY. I do! . . . I got near a grand for the down payment already! (*Puts notice in his back pocket.*)

GERTRUDE. You got that much?!

HARRY. Hell yes! I didn't go throwing it around this trip!

GERTRUDE. There'll be all kinds of problems . . .

HARRY. I can handle 'em, I'm going to talk to Hank in the morning . . .

GERTRUDE. (*Irritated.*) Sure! He'll grab your money, why not, he wants to dump it!!

HARRY. I got it all worked out . . .

GERTRUDE. (*Angry.*) You'll be stuck with a lot of scrap!! (*Takes her cup, cookies, crosses to downstage center table, sits.*) . . . You'll get sick of it . . . and besides, what about your going out to sea!

HARRY. What sea? . . . Those lousy rust buckets I end up on? . . . everything's falling apart, I'm down in the engine room, stuck in that hole all day . . . changing zinc plates on condensers, getting down in the bilges, crawling around in the grease 'n' muck, packing valves, tearing down pumps . . .

GERTRUDE. Poor thing!

HARRY. (*Coffee cup in hand, he crosses to her.*) Sure! . . . I get above deck, I have a chance to sit on the fan tail . . . then I feel like I'm at sea . . . (*Sits next to her.*) and it won't be like giving it all up, I'll still have my own boat.

GERTRUDE. Give it a few days first . . .

HARRY. No! I'm doing it! (*Sips his coffee.*)

GERTRUDE. (*Grudgingly gives in to his determination, too tired to argue over it. Throughout she eats cookies and sips her coffee.*) Well . . . you'll be staying here, so that won't cost you anything, it might work out okay, now look, I'll back you till you get started, but you get in real trouble, you dump her, and I'll do all the talking!

HARRY. No! This is going to be different! I'm going to handle the whole thing by myself! I'm not using your dough this time . . . I'll talk to him! And don't worry, I won't act hungry for it.

GERTRUDE. You don't have a head for business, we could get it for a song!

HARRY. I don't want to hit the man over the head for it, Hank's not a bad guy . . . I know what she's worth.

GERTRUDE. (*Weary.*) Okay . . . but I look the papers over before you sign.

HARRY. (*A beat, then.*) Yeah, yeah . . . ya look the papers over . . . (*Pats her bottom with his foot. Laughs.*) ya happy now?! (*Irritated, she gets up, goes behind bar for a cigarette. He follows.*) Ahhh, look, it's going to work . . . (*With growing excitement.*) See, I hoist 'er out and re-rig her. And you're right it's going to be one hell of a big job, but the hull's in good shape and that's the main thing . . . (*She has crossed back, sits, lights her cigarette.* HARRY *leans on her chair.*) I checked it out when he had it careened last year. And she's toting a couple of Gray engines . . . I know those babies like the back of my hand! (*Moves stage right.*) I get her all decked out . . . and then I'm gonna paint her an off-white, with a deep red stripe going all around the hull. (*He has moved back to her.*) And then I'm takin' her way up the coast. See I figure I can really make a . . .

GERTRUDE. Up the coast?

HARRY. Yeah, Vallejo . . . I can make a good buck there . . . (*Picks up his coffee cup.*)

GERTRUDE. (*Taken aback.*) Vallejo! . . . What do you want to go up there for? What's wrong with right here?!?

HARRY. (*Realizing he's ahead of himself and finding his predicament humorous. Smiles.*) Well . . . nothin' . . .

GERTRUDE. You wouldn't even be staying here . . . it takes the better part of a day just to get there . . .

HARRY. (*Sipping his coffee, he crosses up right, grins.*) I didn't think of that . . .

GERTRUDE. You can't save money that way, paying rent . . . you'd have to live aboard and that's no way!

HARRY. I know . . . (*Laughs.*) I'm not thinking . . .

GERTRUDE. Business'd be just as good right here!

HARRY. Hell, yes!

GERTRUDE. (*Believing he was just carried away.*) You okay?

HARRY. (*Turns, looks at her.*) No . . . (*Smiles.*) I'm not!

GERTRUDE. (*Laughs.*) You're a crazy man!

HARRY. (*He crosses back to her, puts his cup down.*) Yeah! . . . Hey Gert . . . (*Picks up his whisky, toasts.*) To our new boat! (*Drinks.*)

GERTRUDE. Our boat?! I thought I wasn't helping you!

HARRY. You're not, I'm giving ya half anyway, out of my goodness! (*Hands her the glass for her to drink too.*)

GERTRUDE. (*She sets the glass down.*) You're crazier than ever! (*Laughs.*)

HARRY. (*Amazed that she's so perceptive. He leans towards her.*) Am I? . . . Can ya tell? . . . I mean I'm different this trip, right? . . . What . . . what's different about me??

GERTRUDE. I don't know . . .

HARRY. (*Sits down.*) Something happened to me!

GERTRUDE. What?

HARRY. Awhile back . . . I get relieved off the mid-watch, and I come topside out of that stinking hot engine room . . . I open the hatch . . . and I feel strange . . . (*Laughs.*) it's hard to explain . . . I remember the sea was so calm that night, I mean, not a ripple. It doesn't happen too often, the sight is unbelievable if you've never seen it before . . . can you imagine . . . an ocean, an ocean! As far as you can see, that looks like a sheet of glass, like you could walk out on it. The moon up full . . . the sky, not a cloud . . . just all freckled up, with tiny little diamonds . . . all the years I been steaming I never seen anything like it . . . not like that night . . . well, I walked aft and I sat down on number four davit . . . I could feel the screw humming under me . . . (*Makes humming noise.*) and I sat there, watching our wake cutting through this glazed sheet of ice . . . And I started thinking of a kid . . . ya see. I imagined myself sitting there with a little boy next to me . . . and he was my son . . . and it was so real I could see him. He had a tiny pair of non-skids on, and khakis, and a little striped sweater, I remember it was blue. And he had on one of my old watch caps, it was cut down and pulled over his ears to keep out the night cold. And he was sitting on a cushion next to me and I had my arm around him and I was tellin' him all about the sea and everything . . . you know I must have sat there for over an hour just talkin' to him . . . and that's when I started making my plans . . . ya see, I want that kid! And I want my own boat, that's why it's so important I talk to Hank, so I don't have to be away from him so long. And I'd like to get an old beat-up house somewhere, that way it would be cheap, and I could fix it up. And when he gets old enough, I want him to go out with me . . . on the boat, and his old man will teach him how to be the best damn little salt! (*He leans toward her. Smiles.*) And he'll have a great mom! (*A moment.*) Well . . . what do ya think?!

GERTRUDE. (*A moment, then:*) I think you're full of shit! (*Laughs. Gets up, takes her coffee cup, cookies, goes behind bar stage left.*)

HARRY. (*Taken aback.*) I'm full of shit? . . . I tried to tell ya how I feel about a little kid and ya tell me I'm full of shit? . . . that's not funny! (*He gets up, crosses to bar.*) Look, you don't understand . . . let me finish telling ya . . .

GERTRUDE. No! I don't want to hear anymore crap about kids and that sentimental crud!! (*Puts cookies back in tin.*)

HARRY. It's not crud!

GERTRUDE. Well, I don't want to hear it!!

HARRY. If I can't tell ya how I feel, then what's the use to anything?!

GERTRUDE. (*Angry.*) Well, feel something else!! (*HARRY turns away in disgust, crosses back to table, takes pour spout out of bottle and pours himself a shot, GERTRUDE watches him.*) Bring that bottle over here! You drank enough!!

HARRY. I'll pay ya for it! (*Downs the shot. With bottle and glass he starts crossing upstage right, to window.*)

GERTRUDE. You couldn't begin to pay me for all the booze you sopped down around here!!

HARRY. (*He stops, looks at her.*) Oh . . . and I don't do nothing for it?! (*Crosses to bar.*) I'm always working around here, helping out, fixing stuff . . . (*Gesturing upstairs.*) not counting the work I do upstairs in that bed!!

GERTRUDE. (*Glares at him, then with quiet intensity.*)

Oh . . . that's work, is it?! (*He doesn't answer.*) . . . Is it?!!?

HARRY. No! . . . (*Crosses to center table.*) you just boiled me, that's all! (*Sits, pours another shot.*)

GERTRUDE. Moving in here was your idea remember?! . . . help out, earn your keep is all I said! That *other* help I don't need, I do okay!!!

HARRY. Calm down!! . . . I just don't like being laughed at, that's all, by you or anyone! (*Pouring another shot, downs it.*)

GERTRUDE. (*Watching him, a beat, then:*) You're gulping it like a bum . . . what's the matter with you? (*Orders.*) Bring that bottle over here! (*He doesn't respond. Then, almost gently.*) Harry . . . come on . . . bring it over.

HARRY. (*A moment, then, picking up the bottle and glass, crosses stage right end of bar.*) Why'd ya laugh at me? (*Sits.*)

GERTRUDE. (*Feeling a little guilty for putting him down so hard. Says almost gently:*) I'm just tired . . . I get a little silly, that's all. I had a long night . . . (*Remaining behind the bar she moves to sink, near HARRY.*) then you coming in late like this, and all the things you're going to do, you wear me out! (*Takes dirty glasses off bar, puts them in sink, washes them.*)

HARRY. But I make sense, don't I? I mean it's not like the truck, I know I hated that damn thing!

GERTRUDE. And you never finished paying me for it either!

HARRY. I know, I will, I intend to!

GERTRUDE. But you gave it away to one of your buddies! Eight hundred bucks! A month in the moving business!

HARRY. I was mixed up at the time, I got it straight now. It took a lot of figuring! (*He has poured himself a shot, and is downing it.*)

GERTRUDE. (*Goes to take the bottle.*) That's enough of that!

HARRY. (*Not letting her have it.*) I still got the chills!

GERTRUDE. Give me the bottle!

HARRY. I'm shakin' all over . . . I'm okay . . . (*A moment, then:*) . . . Ya see . . . when a reciprocating pump broke aboard ship, I said . . .

GERTRUDE. (*She lets go the bottle.*) Look, I'm tired! (*Crosses stage left end of bar, picks up dirty beer mugs.*)

HARRY. Let me tell ya this one thing . . . (*He crosses behind the bar stage left.*)

GERTRUDE. (*Back at sink now.*) No! . . . In the morning, okay?!

HARRY. Ya see I said to myself . . .

GERTRUDE. (*Angrily, cuts him off.*) Just let me get cleaned up here! Then we'll get some sleep!! We're both too tired to make any sense right now!!

HARRY. (*Disgusted, he puts the bottle on bar, then, glass in hand, he starts up the stairs, he stops, leans on wall.*) When we go upstairs tonight . . . and I get in that sack, ya know what's going to happen?! (*She doesn't answer, her back to him, she busily washes glasses.*) . . . I'm going to take all my clothes off!

GERTRUDE. (*Matter of factly.*) Well I certainly hope so.

HARRY. I'm gonna lean over to ya . . . and I'm gonna put my *big* . . . (*He stops. Watches her intently. She continues washing, he finally sees her smile.*) arms! . . . around ya . . . (GERTRUDE *is grinning now, busily washing. He says sexily:*) and I'm gonna run my tongue all the way down your back . . . I'm gonna make little circles on your belly . . . I'm gonna blow hot air in your ear . . . and then I'm gonna say . . . you know when that reciprocating pump broke aboard ship?

GERTRUDE. (*Turning to him.*) Oh no, you're not!

HARRY. . . . You don't want that, do ya?

GERTRUDE. No! . . . I do not want that!

HARRY. (*Smiles.*) Well, don't ya think I better tell ya about it now then?

GERTRUDE. (*Dries her hands.*) Yeah, I think you better tell me about it now!

HARRY. (*Smiling, he comes down the stairs, sets his glass on the bar.*) Well ya see, we had this old beat up pump aboard ship, and it kept breaking down . . . (*Since she has to listen, and wanting to get comfortable, she crosses, sits on bar stool stage right.* HARRY *has crossed, stands next to her.*) and it wouldn't work . . . (*He demonstrates.*) I mean it would pump *up* okay, but I had to stand over her and push her *down*. Ya see, the sleeves were worn almost clean through . . . and there's no parts to fix 'er. (*Laughs.*) Hell, come on! I mean I'm not an idiot . . . I'm not going to stand over an old pump all day and keep shoving her down! But the bilges were filling up, everything's leaking, see . . . and that reciprocating pump was the only one still working. So come on, what would you do? . . . What would anyone do? . . . You'd weigh 'er down, right?!

GERTRUDE. (*Amusing herself, not knowing what he's talking about.*) Right! That's what I'd do!

HARRY. (*He crosses down right center, demonstrates the following.*) Sure you would! . . . So I got me a pail, and I filled it with some pipe, and I hooked 'er on!

GERTRUDE. Exactly!

HARRY. What do you mean, that's crazy!

GERTRUDE. Of course!

HARRY. I mean, the weight would push the pump down okay . . . but you'd have to pull the bucket off so she could pump back!

GERTRUDE. Right!

HARRY. But I figured I'd give it a try anyway!

GERTRUDE. Why not?

HARRY. So I put the bucket on old Mom . . . yeah, I used to call her old Mom . . . so I hook 'er on . . . and she works! . . . (*Clenching his fists, raising and lowering his arms he becomes a human pump.*) I mean she's a pumping *up* and *down* . . . cleaning out the bilges. (*Laughs.*) It was the craziest thing don't ya see

. . . all that weight must have tightened 'er up . . . you should have seen old Mom a pumping!

GERTRUDE. (*Starts to get up.*) Is that it?

HARRY. (*Runs to her.*) Almost! . . . so ya see, the only time I thought I couldn't solve something in the engine room . . . I really did . . . and I said to myself, "Harry, why can't you always do that . . . you know, solve things?" And then I started thinking about us . . . (*Sits next to her.*) and I solved that, too!

GERTRUDE. Solved what?

HARRY. What we're going to do!

GERTRUDE. And what's that?

HARRY. We're going to Vallejo! (*She laughs.*) It's all set!

GERTRUDE. (*Gets up, crosses to sink.*) . . . Uh huh . . . well, that's good! I was wondering where I was going!

HARRY. (*Crosses to her.*) I'm serious about this now!

GERTRUDE. I'll pack tonight!

HARRY. (*Standing behind her he puts his arms around her waist. Laughs.*) Good . . . now let me finish telling ya . . .

GERTRUDE. (*Sternly.*) That's all! You said after the pumping story!

HARRY. It's not a *story!* We're getting out of here, you and me!

GERTRUDE. I'm losing my patience now! (*Crosses with several clean coffee cups left end of bar. HARRY, right behind her.*)

HARRY. Look, if you don't come with me, I'll have to go without ya!!

GERTRUDE. Okay! (*Puts cups under counter. Starts to cross from behind bar.*)

HARRY. (*Taking her arm, stopping her.*) Wait a minute! What do you mean, *okay!* (*Smiles.*) . . . you care about me, you're not letting me go anywhere!

GERTRUDE. You're drunk! (*She pulls away, takes his*

whisky bottle off bar, crosses to downstage center table. Puts pour spout back.)

HARRY. Oh, yeah?!? . . . Then why ya always tricking me?! . . . (*She looks at him, not understanding.*) Yeah, I found out . . . last year one of the guys told ya to tell me personally, when I came in, they wanted to sign me on. (*Knowing now what he means, she evades the issue. Picks up his coffee cup, goes behind bar, puts cup in sink, bottle back on shelf. He follows.*) There were friends of mine on that ship . . . knew I needed a job bad and were jumping the list for me. (*Wanting to get away from him she crosses back to the table, wipes it off. He crosses to her.*) You asked them for how long, remember? . . . You found out I was going to be away for six months, you never told me. (*She crosses, wipes off upstage right table.*) I came in that same night and asked if you had anything for me, you looked at me stone-faced, you said "nothing." That ship got underway the next morning and I stayed here working for you . . . and you don't care?!?

GERTRUDE. (*Wiping off downstage right table. She notices a puddle of water on the floor.*) Will ya look at that . . . this damn rain! The roof is leaking so I put some pans out upstairs, they must be running over, it's coming down here now.

HARRY. (*Crosses to her.*) What about that time!

GERTRUDE. It's like a river up there! . . . My bed got soaked, I had to bring the mattress down, dry it out . . . I been sleeping out back for a week now . . .

HARRY. I'm talking to you!

GERTRUDE. You think you could fix it?

HARRY. (*Moves away. A beat, then:*) You're right! I'm a crazy man! Crazy to be hanging around here! I can go anywhere! Do anything! Have any babe! (*Sits on bar stool stage right.*) I'm a good-looking guy! I was never seen without a doll of a broad, never! I could pick 'em up ten minutes after we hit the beach! "Hey! There goes Harry, fix me up, ol' buddy!"

GERTRUDE. (*Crosses, goes behind bar.*) With a dose!

HARRY. I could pick up anything!

GERTRUDE. (*Hangs up rag.*) I seen you with some of your . . . *anythings!*

HARRY. (*Turns away.*) Ahhhh what do you know . . . my buddies think I'm sharp!

GERTRUDE. (*Moves to him, leans on bar.*) You been away . . . you got a lot of plans again. You're antsy, that's all. Think I don't get that way? . . . I see 'em steaming in . . . going out . . . hear 'em tying up in the morning . . . dropping the gang plank . . . calling down chow . . . think I don't get antsy? (*Looks at him, a moment, then:*) . . . You're tired, help me get out the mattress.

HARRY. . . . The mattress?

GERTRUDE. Yeah! (*She turns off the Ballantine Beer sign above juke box.*)

HARRY. What ya talking about? . . . what mattress?

GERTRUDE. (*She turns off the two fluorescent lights.*) I told you, I got a river up there, I been sleeping out back! (*Crosses to the back room, but stops as he says:*)

HARRY. You been sleepin' on that rotten deck back there?

GERTRUDE. Uh-huh.

HARRY. Did ya know the guys are afraid to go back there to take a leak; that some rat'll chop it off, and you're sleeping back there?

GERTRUDE. You going to help me or not?

HARRY. I'll bet you really give the longshoremen a treat in the morning . . . peeking in on you in the raw!

GERTRUDE. I got the window fixed.

HARRY. Oh yeah?? . . . Well, you better move up on the bar . . . 'cause those big-ass rats'll nibble your ears! (*Laughs.*)

GERTRUDE. (*Crossing to him.*) That's better, I like you laughing! . . . Come on . . . I want some more!

HARRY. (*Stops laughing.*) No, you ain't getting any more.

GERTRUDE. (*Tickles him.*) Give me some more! (*Another tickle. Laughing,* HARRY *jumps up, she tickles him as they move stage right. She stops, pleased he's out of his mood.*)

HARRY. You know what I'm laughing at? . . . You! 'Cause you're all dirty . . . and you got cake in your hair. (*Laughs. He crosses to coat rack.* GERTRUDE *sits at bar, right.*) And you sleep with rats! (*He is a little high and having a great time.*) Ol' Dirty Gerty! (*Takes a cigar out of his jacket, unwraps it as he sings:*) Big ol' Dirty Gerty . . . she runs a . . .

GERTRUDE. What are you singing?

HARRY. (*Crosses left, goes behind bar.*) The song. (*He hums. Takes a box of matches from under the counter.*)

GERTRUDE. What song?

HARRY. The song all the guys sing! (*He lights his cigar.*)

GERTRUDE. (*Fascinated.*) Is it about me?

HARRY. Yeah, you heard it!

GERTRUDE. No! What do they sing about me? (*Gets up, crosses to him.*)

HARRY. (*Laughs. Puts the matches away.*) Aw, come on! You musta heard the guys singing it!

GERTRUDE. No, I haven't!

HARRY. (*Stares at her, realizing she hasn't heard it, grimaces.*) Oh shit!

GERTRUDE. Look . . . I know they all talk about me . . . (*She moves toward him.*) for Christ's sake, it's good business to have 'em talking . . . (*As she starts to go behind the bar he runs right, she cuts him off, grabs the blanket.*) I just didn't know they were singing!

HARRY. (*Serious.*) They're not.

GERTRUDE. (*Chuckles.*) I want to hear it, it'll be fun! (*Drags him to one of the bar stools, stage right, sits.*)

HARRY. Are you sure?

GERTRUDE. Yeah! Come on!!

HARRY. (*A beat, then:*) I don't know all the words!

(*He runs upstage right,* GERTRUDE, *hanging on the blanket, goes with him.*)

GERTRUDE. (*Laughs.*) You remember it . . . how's it go?

HARRY. . . . Okay, but you stop me if you don't like it?!

GERTRUDE. Yeah, yeah, go ahead! (*Not letting go the blanket, she sits at table.*)

HARRY.
Big Ol' Dirty Gerty . . .

is that okay?

GERTRUDE. (*Smiling.*) That's okay!

HARRY.
She runs a bar down by the docks,
It's not made of wood, nor made of rocks,
It's built with cow dung!

That's *still* okay?

GERTRUDE. Yeah! That's still okay! (*She lets go the blanket. Confident now,* HARRY *continues.* GERTRUDE *laughs throughout the song, loving it.*)

HARRY.
You walk right in and fall through the floor,
Pick yourself up asking for more,
Move to the bar and say anyone home.

Then a rumble is heard from the ol' back room,
And Gerty appears swinging a broom,
Chasing a rat half frightened to death.

She waddles right up and pours ya a slug,
Her sweat dripping in your nice fresh mug.

That's Two Ton Dirty Gerty,
She makes me laugh, she makes me sad,
Takes my money, but I'm always glad,

Makes me forget all my trouble and strife,
Makes me forget of ever taking a wife.

And after closing up at night,
She kicks ya out in the dawning light.
Worn and weary from many a fight,
She waddles upstairs two tons of might,
A chocolate cake right at her side,
　　(*Sexily, moving his hips.*)
And if she likes ya special, she'll give ya a ride!

GERTRUDE. (*Laughing, she applauds. Crosses to* HARRY *who has moved near the juke box.*) Bravo! . . . Harry, you're crazy! (*Puts her arms around him.*)

HARRY. (*Laughing.*) I didn't make it up . . . it was those loony buddies of mine!

GERTRUDE. (*She puts his hands on her waist to do a little Conga line.*) How does it go? . . . (*He throws his cigar in the sink. They both start singing different verses of the song, both having a great time, moving downstage right. She turns to him, they kiss warmly. Then she says.*) Harry . . . dance with me. (*They dance very slowly for a few moments, then:*)

HARRY. I think I'm a little drunk . . .

GERTRUDE. All we need is some music . . . (*Starts crossing to the stairwell.*) I'll go get the phonograph. It's my favorite record and I never played it for ya before. (*Up the stairs now, she exits.*)

HARRY. I don't wanna dance! . . . Gertrude? (*He crosses to stairwell.*) I don't wanna dance . . . (*Laughs.*) I wanna drink! (*Behind the bar, he starts to take a glass, stops, getting an idea. Not wanting* GERTRUDE *to know that he's drinking, he takes a coffee cup, fills it with whisky. Sings:*)
She likes ya special . . . she'll give ya a ride . . . (*Calls upstairs.*) I'm special . . . right, Gert? (*Puts the bottle back. Suddenly depressed. Quietly says.*) yeah . . . I'm special! . . . I hate that song! (*Coffee cup in hand he crosses slowly to upstage right table. Then, looks*

toward the stairwell.) Why can't I talk to you? . . . Not
just joking around 'n' laughing . . . but real talk . . .
(*Drinks a good amount of the whisky, then sits.* GER-
TRUDE *enters, carrying a phonograph and record. Moves
to left end of bar as:*)

GERTRUDE. Ya know . . . I wish I could have been
a dancer . . . (*She puts phonograph on bar. Plugs it in.*
HARRY *leans across the table, resting his head on his arms.
Concentrated on what she's doing, she doesn't notice
this.*) they seem so graceful . . . they kind of float, ya
know . . . (*Puts on the record.*) like their feet don't
touch . . . it just fascinates me . . . (*The music plays;
it is:* Cajita de Musica, *"Little Music Box." She adjusts
the volume.*) come on, dance with me . . . (*Now, sees
him slumped over on the table. A moment, then before
she can turn the phonograph off, the music moves in on
her. She listens, lost a little in the gentleness of the chords.
Then she sways and lifts her arms, doing little dance
steps as a child might. Unseen by* GERTRUDE, HARRY *has
opened his eyes and is watching her. She turns slowly as
a figure on a music box, until she sees him looking at
her. Embarrassed, she laughs, curtsies.*) Dance with me.

HARRY. (*He lifts his head. Moved at seeing this sensitive side of* GERTRUDE, *says warmly.*) That was beautiful
. . . that was just beautiful . . .

GERTRUDE. (*Smiles, crosses to him, takes his hand.*)
Come on, let's dance!

HARRY. (*Gently.*) In a minute, okay? . . . Sit down
first . . . (*She sits next to him. He gets up, crosses to
phonograph, turns it off. A beat, then:*) I'm a dummy,
right? . . . I'm a dummy! I mean what do I know?

GERTRUDE. (*Compassionately.*) A lot of things! . . .
You're a good carpenter, a good engineer . . . (*Smiles.*)
and you're about to be a good roof-fixer, right?

HARRY. (*Crosses back to her.*) No, I mean other stuff!
. . . *you!* . . . I'm dumb about you! . . . over a year
I've been staying with ya now, and I don't know ya . . .
you never tell me nothing!

GERTRUDE. (*A moment, then:*) Well . . . I was born . . . right here. In the Sea Horse . . .

HARRY. Oh, yeah?!

GERTRUDE. Tending bar! (*Laughs.*) There I was, just toddling around in my diapers, pourin' 'em out and kickin' 'em out!

HARRY. (*Laughs.*) Oh yeah! . . . well I ain't that dumb . . . I know you was married once . . .

GERTRUDE. (*A moment, then:*) Who told you that?

HARRY. (*Hoping she will take this lead and talk about herself.*) One of the guys said ya was hitched a long time ago.

GERTRUDE. (*Quiet warning.*) Ya *hear* . . . a lot of things.

HARRY. (*Disappointed, but not wanting to press it.*) . . . Naw . . . that was all. (*Finishes his whisky. A beat, then:*) Remember the first day I came in this place? (*Sits next to her.*) I had this babe with me . . . you said "Leave the bitch outside, Handsome, and come on in!" My babe says "Honey, let's get out of here, that woman scares me!" You said "It's a house rule sailor, nothing through that door without balls, come back without the whore sometime, and the first drink'll be on me!" (*Laughs.*) . . . What a way to talk . . .

GERTRUDE. (*Smiles, gets up, moves behind him.*) You came back alright . . . that same night!

HARRY. I never had that much fun in my life!

GERTRUDE. (*Rubs his neck.*) Everyone sure took to you . . .

HARRY. How could they miss! . . . You said it was a rule for me to buy everyone a first drink . . . you nearly broke me!

GERTRUDE. Well, they took to ya, didn't they?!? (*Smiles. Puts her arms around him.*) . . . You know . . . that was the first time I brought anyone upstairs, the same night I met 'em.

HARRY. Yeah?

GERTRUDE. Uh-huh.

HARRY. It was kind of funny . . . I mean you wasn't my type!

GERTRUDE. (*Chuckles.*) I'll bet!

HARRY. I remember I said to myself . . . "Harry . . . you don't do it right, you could get killed."

GERTRUDE. (*Laughs.*) . . . You did it right!

HARRY. Yeah, lucky for me I did it right! (*He takes her hand.*) . . . Gertrude? . . . do you ever hear things talk? . . . Not people, *things* . . . machines 'n' water 'n' wind 'n' stuff. (*She realizes that he's been drinking again, sniffs his coffee cup.*) Ya know what a shaft alley is?

GERTRUDE. I told you, no more booze!! (*Crosses, goes behind bar, puts cup in sink.*)

HARRY. Ya know what a shaft alley is?! (*Disgusted, as she takes his wet cigar out of sink, throws it in garbage pail. He gets up, crosses to her.*) I go down this ladder, see . . . (*Although a little high, he is still articulate, not slurring his words.*) Way down below the water line . . . (GERTRUDE *goes to refrigerator, pours a glass of soda.*) and there's the shaft . . . it turns the screw . . . the propeller. (*Sits center bar.*) And I go down there to check the bearings . . . and it's quiet down there . . . and I like to sit for a bit, alone, and think. I like to listen to the shaft . . . it talks.

GERTRUDE. (*She has taken off the record and unplugged the phonograph, winds up the cord.*) It does what?

HARRY. (*Smiles.*) It talks! . . . I mean it rumbles . . . It's rusty in places and it squeaks . . . and it kinda says stuff . . . like . . . (*Gesturing with his hand, indicating the turning shaft and making a squeaking sound.*) "I'm old . . . I'm old" and I'd answer 'n' say "Oh, yeah . . . oh, yeah." (GERTRUDE, *leaning on stage left end of bar, drinks some soda, begins to get caught up in what he's saying.*) . . . then she'd speed up 'n' say other things, like . . . (*Again gestures.*) "I'm so long at sea, I'm so long at sea" and I'd answer, 'n' say "Your bearings'll be fine, your bearings'll be fine" . . . and then,

that strange night, you know, the one I told ya about,
the glass ocean . . . well, later that same night, I went
down to the shaft alley, to think about it. And that old
shaft is rumbling away again, and this time, she's saying
"Gertrude Blum . . . Gertrude Blum" . . . and I started
saying it "Gertrude Blum . . . Gertrude Blum" . . . but
then she starts speeding up, and my saying "Gertrude
Blum" . . . doesn't fit the rumble . . . and it started
saying . . . (*Indicates the speed of the shaft, spinning his
arm rapidly, and talking with compulsive intensity.*) "I
love Gertrude Blum, I love Gertrude Blum" and I started
sayin' it— (*Moving toward her.*)

HARRY.	GERTRUDE.
"I love Gertrude Blum,	Shut up!!
I love Gertrude Blum,	You drunken damn fool,
I love Gertrude Blum,	shut up!!!
I love Gertrude Blum"	I SAID SHUT UP!!!!!!
	(*Throws the soda in his face.*)

GERTRUDE. You *are* a crazy man!! The guys hear you
spouting that love stuff at me they'll laugh you off the
pier!

HARRY. (*Angry, wiping his face, with the blanket.*)
They won't hear it! . . . none of 'em will hear it! . . .
We'll be way up the coast, where nobody knows us! They
can't laugh at me!!! (*A moment, then he smiles.*) You
see . . . I figured it all . . . How in the hell can they
possibly laugh at me, if we ain't here!

GERTRUDE. (*Trying to make sense out of what he's
saying.*) Vallejo?!

HARRY. (*He makes his way to downstage center table.*)
You got it!

GERTRUDE. Is that what this is all about? . . . You
wanna run away with me?

HARRY. (*Happy she understands it.*) That's it! (*Sits.*)
GERTRUDE. Why?
HARRY. Because I love you!! (*She stares at him in-*

credulously.) I know! . . . I couldn't believe it myself!
. . . But it all fits don't ya see . . .

GERTRUDE. . . . The machine's been telling ya!

HARRY. (*Realization*.) . . . yeah . . . kinda . . .

GERTRUDE. . . . The still ocean . . . and the pumps
. . . the shaft . . .

HARRY. (*Fondly*.) Ahhh, the shaft . . .

GERTRUDE. (*Crosses to him*.) And your buddies won't
know . . .

HARRY. That's right, they won't know!

GERTRUDE. You wanna hide me! (*Both roar with
laughter*.)

HARRY. Yeah!! (*Realizing what he said*.) I mean no
. . . I mean . . .

GERTRUDE. You mean I'm a blubberball and you
wanna hide me! (*Both laugh. During the following she
moves from his left side to his right, back and forth*.)

HARRY. . . . It's just that . . .

GERTRUDE. I been sleeping around so you wanna hide
me . . .

HARRY. No, that's . . .

GERTRUDE. And all your buddies know!

HARRY. (*Still laughing*.) They won't find out! . . . I
mean . . . you're mixing me up . . .

GERTRUDE. You wanna hide me!!

HARRY. (*Suddenly explodes, jumps up, his fist
clenched*.) Quit making fun of me!!!

GERTRUDE. (*Glares at him*.) You don't have any balls,
Harry, you belong in a dress! Who'd wanna run away
with you! (*She turns, goes behind bar*.)

HARRY. (*Infuriated, goes after her. Slams his fist on
the bar*.) YOU DAMN LARD ASS!!!!! SHUT UP!!!!!
. . . You're right! I was just kidding ya!! . . . I been
using ya, my buddies all know it!!! . . . Staying here
free!! . . . Drinking your booze!! . . . Banging ya
when I get the notion!! Who'd wanna run away with a
fat pig like you!!!!! (GERTRUDE *has moved right end
of bar. Slowly he moves toward her now as:*) You're a

lard ass full of hate!! . . . You hate everything!!!
Ohhhh, you hate my son! Ya hate little kids!! (*Right up
to her.*) . . . You are so full of hate!! (GERTRUDE *at-
tacks him viciously with her fists. HARRY, forced back,
near downstage center table, drops to his knees, tries to
protect himself. Covers his head.*)

HARRY. Stop it!!! Stop it!!! Damn you!! Stop hitting me!!! Quit hitting!!!	GERTRUDE. You damn son of a bitch!!! Who the hell do you think you are!!!! You bastard!! You damn bastard!!!!!

HARRY. (*Swings wildly, hitting GERTRUDE with a
tremendous blow to the stomach.*) QUIT HITTING!!!!!
(*She falls to the floor in agony, her breath knocked out
by HARRY's punch. She clutches her stomach, desperately
trying to breathe. HARRY, hands over head, confused,
not knowing or seeing what he has done, has crawled
away from her. Realizing she has stopped hitting him:*)
What ya trying to do?! Knock my head off?!! You
crazy woman . . . (*Seeing her now, writhing on the
floor . . . Starting to get her breath back, she moans in
pain. He shakily gets up, moves toward her.*) Hey . . .
what's the matter . . . (*Bending over her, seeing she is
in terrible agony.*) what happened! . . . I hit ya?!

GERTRUDE. . . . My belly . . . oh, my belly . . . you
hurt my belly . . .

HARRY. (*Distressed, he tries to comfort her.*) Oh . . .
I'm sorry I'm so sorry . . . It was an accident . . .

GERTRUDE. (*Gaining a little vocal strength.*) You hurt
me . . . you hurt me . . .

HARRY. I'm sorry . . . I never hit a woman before! . . .

GERTRUDE. (*She clutches her stomach.*) Is there blood
on me?!?

HARRY. What . . .

GERTRUDE. Blood!! Is there blood on me?!! Am I
bleeding?!?!

HARRY. (*On his knees, next to her now, he sees there is*

no blood.) . . . No! . . . there's no blood! . . . I just knocked the wind . . .

GERTRUDE. (*Panicked, she screams.*) You hurt me! I'm bleeding . . . you hurt me!! (*She starts swinging wildly.*)

HARRY. (*Trying desperately to hold her down.*) What's the matter!?! Hey!!! Take it easy!!!!

GERTRUDE. (*Screams.*) YOU HURT ME!! GET AWAY FROM ME!!! YOU HURT ME!! SOMEBODY HELP ME!!! YOU HURT ME!!!

HARRY. (*Panicked.*) I WON'T HIDE YA!! I'M NOT GONNA HIDE YA!!! I LOVE YA!!! YOU'RE NOT A LARD ASS!!!

HARRY. I'M NOT GONNA HIDE YA!!! I WON'T HIDE YA!!! I'M NOT GONNA HIDE YA!!!

END OF ACT ONE

ACT TWO

*Lights come up. It is 11:00 A.M. the following morning,
the sound of a soft rain can be heard. The bar is
empty, a pot of oatmeal is cooking on the hot plate,
on back counter, stage left. A pot of coffee is also
on.* HARRY'S *sea bag, used as a pillow, and the blanket*
GERTRUDE *gave him last night, are sprawled out
downstage right, his boots are near the downstage
right table. He has spread newspapers under the
makeshift bed to help keep out the dampness.* HARRY
*enters, comes down the stairwell with a pail of water.
He has changed to a red plaid shirt, the same
gabardine pants and is wearing white sweat socks.
He puts the pail under the bar. He moves to the
stove and notices the oatmeal is burning. He pulls
the pot off, wraps a rag around the handle and stirs
it up hoping it's not too bad. Preoccupied, he is un-
aware that* GERTRUDE *enters from the back room.
She has changed into a dress, it is old fashioned and
a bit snug. Her hair is down. He takes two bowls
from the back counter. As he turns to put them on
the bar he sees* GERTRUDE.

HARRY. Oh . . . morning . . . (*Seeing how pretty she
looks.*) Wow!

GERTRUDE. (*Uncomfortable.*) Forgot I had this outfit.
(*She crosses to bar.*)

HARRY. I got it out of that box near the stove . . . I
pressed it up and set it out for ya . . . I was hoping
you'd want it.

GERTRUDE. You didn't give me much choice . . . you
pulled my clothes off and stuffed 'em in a pail of water.

HARRY. Your things were kinda . . . I figured they
could use a soak.

GERTRUDE. (*A beat, then indicating his cooking.*) You've been busy.

HARRY. Yeah, I burned the oatmeal a little, but nothing serious. (*Takes plate from back counter, covers oatmeal.*)

GERTRUDE. Where did you find oatmeal?

HARRY. On the window sill in the back . . . I found a pot back there, too.

GERTRUDE. . . . For the birds. (*Crosses, picks up record player.*)

HARRY. What?

GERTRUDE. The birds . . . I've been feeding it to the birds, it's stale.

HARRY. (*Looks in the pot.*) Oh . . . well, it can't hurt us. (*Afterthought.*) How stale is it?

GERTRUDE. (*She has crossed to stairwell, puts record player on stairs.*) It'll be okay . . . here, let me. (HARRY *moves out of her way, sits on bar stool stage left.*) Why didn't you wake me?

HARRY. You were sleeping so deep . . . I figured I could manage.

GERTRUDE. (*Spoons oatmeal into one of the bowls.*) What is that rig back there?

HARRY. It's kind of a hammock . . . only I used the mattress and some rope, I couldn't let ya sleep on that rotten deck . . . I just carried you back and plopped ya in. How is your belly?

GERTRUDE. (*Sharply.*) It's okay! (*She takes oatmeal, spoon, crosses to downstage center table, sets them down. Notices* HARRY *in his stocking feet.*) Where's your boots?

HARRY. I didn't want to wake ya . . . you know, clomping around back there.

GERTRUDE. (*Indicating* HARRY's *makeshift bed.*) Slept there?

HARRY. (*Crosses near bed.*) Yeah, it was too crowded in the back for the two of us . . . I didn't sleep too good though.

GERTRUDE. (*Goes back behind the bar, pours him a cup of coffee.*) Freezing, huh?

HARRY. No, I was worried about . . . (*He stops as she glares at him, not wanting to discuss last night, or her condition. Sensing this, he says:*) I was just a little jumpy . . . getting back 'n' all. (*Crosses stage right end of bar.*)

GERTRUDE. (*Takes pitcher of milk from refrigerator, puts it on a tray with coffee and bowl of sugar.*) Thought you'd still be sleeping it off, the way you were boozing! (*She crosses to table with tray.*) Come on, sit down and eat!

HARRY. (*He crosses to table, notices she hasn't fixed anything for herself.*) Wait a minute, what about you!

GERTRUDE. I'm not hungry.

HARRY. (*He sits.*) Yo gotta have something in ya!

GERTRUDE. Later. (*Crosses behind bar.*)

HARRY. (*Stares at his oatmeal.*) You gonna make me eat this stuff by myself?

GERTRUDE. It's okay!

HARRY. Well, sit down at least, keep me company . . . (*He pulls a chair around for her to sit. GERTRUDE crosses to the table. HARRY sticks the spoon straight up in his oatmeal, lets it go, it doesn't move.*) I think this stuff has set.

GERTRUDE. (*Gets up.*) I'll get ya some flakes.

HARRY. No, no, sit down . . . sit down! Don't bother, I'll eat later when you get hungry. (*GERTRUDE sits, looking at him quizzically, irritated at all this attention. He smiles.*) I can't get over it . . . you look beautiful! (*GERTRUDE pulls her hair back, starts to put a rubber band around it, that she had on her wrist.*) What ya doing? (*Stopping her.*) Don't do that, it looks so pretty down!

GERTRUDE. (*Angry.*) Cut it out! (*Gets up, goes behind the bar, continues fixing her hair as:*) What is all this crap?!? . . . You got me hanging up in the air back there! . . . you cook my bird seed! . . . you've been fussing, nosing around, so you belted me one, that mean you gotta please me or something?!!?

HARRY. No, that's . . .

GERTRUDE. Look, don't flatter yourself, I been hit a lot harder!!! . . . I just got a little sick, that's all, so knock it off!!!!

HARRY. Hell, I wasn't . . .

GERTRUDE. Don't scratch! . . . Don't ever scratch!! Not for anyone or anything, without your guts ya go under, I'm telling ya, you do something, it's over, forget it!!! (*Then, almost to herself.*) You start scratching a little, giving a little, then they . . . (*She catches herself.*)

HARRY. (*Unable to tell her that she has misunderstood all his intentions, he tries to connect what she is saying now with what happened last night. A moment, then, with quiet intensity.*) I'll beat the hell out of him!

GERTRUDE. What?

HARRY. The guy that beat you bloody! That's what you meant last night, wasn't it? It wasn't me you was afraid of!

GERTRUDE. (*A beat, then.*) You gonna help me today?

HARRY. (GERTRUDE *reaches for a coffee cup under bar. He crosses to her.*) That guy you was married to, was he the one who hurt you?!

GERTRUDE. (*Viciously, she slams the cup on bar.*) I SAID!!!! (*With frightening intensity.*) . . . Are you going to help me today?

HARRY. . . . Yeah . . . sure . . . I'm gonna help ya . . . (*A moment, then* GERTRUDE *starts coming around stage right end of bar.*) That's my favorite color . . . blue. (*Indicating her dress.*) Know that? I didn't know you liked blue . . . (*Indicating the floral pattern.*) and red . . . I like red.

GERTRUDE. (*Uncomfortable, sits on bar stool her back to him.*) Shows the dirt too easy . . . I'll take it off when my other things dry.

HARRY. No! . . . that looks so nice on ya red and blue!

GERTRUDE. One night in here . . . it'll be all rags.

HARRY. (*He moves to her, points to her dress, gasps.*
GERTRUDE *turns, looks at him.*) And lavender! . . . I'll
bet you didn't know you had lavender on that dress?!
(*She looks down at her dress trying to see where he sees
lavender.*) Right there! (*He gently pokes one of the
floral patterns on the tip of her breast.*)

GERTRUDE. (*Irritated, pushing his hand away.*) Don't
do that!

HARRY. Wait a minute! . . . I think I see a whole
rainbow!! (*Pressing his eye right against her breast, as
if he can see right into it.*) My God!! Will ya look at
that!! . . . Yellow 'n' orange 'n' green 'n' lemon 'n' blue
'n' gold . . . and a guy on a motorcycle! (*She laughs. He
strokes her breasts tenderly.*) And there's a farm with
hills 'n' mountains 'n' trees 'n' ducks . . . and a boy
pickin' blueberries . . . (*She kisses him. He takes her
in his arms, they kiss warmly. A moment, then:*)
That's better . . . (*A beat.*) Come on . . . (*Very sexy,
starting to take her to his bed.*) Come onnnnnnnn . . .

GERTRUDE. (*Laughing.*) Not now . . . I unlock in an
hour, I gotta set up!

HARRY. What do ya have to open today for! We'd have
all day together!! (*Both laugh.*)

GERTRUDE. I can't . . . stop it! . . .

HARRY. Come on, little ducky . . . to the pond! (*He's
making progress in spite of her resistance.*)

GERTRUDE. I can't! . . . Not now!

HARRY. Now, now . . . come on . . . (*Getting her
closer to the bed.*) I'm going to be wonderful!

GERTRUDE. (*Resisting the temptation.*) Please . . . I
want to, but I can't!

HARRY. . . . Fantastic! . . . Incredible! . . . Bril-
liant!!

GERTRUDE. (*Giggles.*) My, my, my, such big words!
(HARRY *is kneeling on the blanket now, she kisses him,
then knocks him over. Laughs.*) Later, I got things to do!
(*Crosses behind the bar.*)

HARRY. (*Sprawled out on the blanket.*) Come back here!

GERTRUDE. No! Now put that stuff away!!

HARRY. (*Laughs.*) Let's mess up the dress!

GERTRUDE. Get your boots on! (*Starts stacking glasses on back shelf, her back to him. A beat, then, HARRY reaches for his sea bag, pulls it alongside him. He strokes the bag tenderly, making sensual sounds, looking at GERTRUDE and trying to get her attention. She does not respond, so he vocalizes his feelings for his bag.*)

HARRY. I love you, bag! (GERTRUDE *is a little surprised and as she turns around, HARRY dives back to his bag. He necks with it, stroking and kissing it.*)

GERTRUDE. (*Irritated.*) Harry, stop it! (*Comes around stage right end of bar, watching him intently. Smiles.*) Come on now, stop it! (*Becoming engrossed.*) Harry, come on now, stop it . . . sssssssssss . . . I love it! Ooo-oooh, I love it!! (*Crosses slowly to him.*) Oh, yes, right there! . . . oh, that's wonderful! Slowly now! . . . oh, that's it, that's it! Gently! Oh, that's beautiful . . . oh, yesssss!! . . . I tell you what, I'll close up early, save it for tonight!

HARRY. (*His endeavor successful, she's within reach, he grabs her, pulling her down on the blanket.*) Gotcha!!! . . . Come here!! (*They laugh. HARRY kisses her long and tenderly. Then, he says warmly.*) I love you, Gert.

GERTRUDE. . . . It's me you're talking to.

HARRY. I mean it.

GERTRUDE. (*Getting uncomfortable, she pulls away.*) Yeah, yeah . . . (*Gets up.*)

HARRY. Wait a minute . . .

GERTRUDE. Let's go!

HARRY. We were so nice 'n' cozy!

GERTRUDE. You gonna move it?!?

HARRY. Okay, that's the way you want it! (*Grabs his sea bag, pulls it close to him.*) Come here, baggy!

GERTRUDE. Give me that!! (*Laughing, HARRY hangs on*

as she pulls the bag, dragging him a few feet. He lets go. She continues crossing upstage right.)

HARRY. (*Warningly.*) Eh! Eh!! Eh!!! (GERTRUDE *stops, looks at him.*) Treat her gentle! (*He laughs.* GERTRUDE *smiles, puts the bag down next to the juke box. During this,* HARRY *jumps up, unlatches the front door, and standing in the open doorway, yells at the top of his lungs.*) I LOVE GERTRUDE BLUM!!!!! YOU HEAR THAT YOU GUYS . . . (*Furious,* GERTRUDE *charges after him.*) I LOVE . . .

GERTRUDE. (*Grabs him by the belt, yanking him into the room.*) For Christ's sake, that's not funny!!! . . . Now get in here!!!! (*Slams the door shut.*) What the hell you doing?!!?

HARRY. (*Crossing to window upstage right.*) I'm letting 'em know how I feel!

GERTRUDE. (*Crossing to him.*) Settle down!!!

HARRY. (*Yells out window.*) I EVEN LOVE HER WHEN SHE'S MAD!!

GERTRUDE. You starting that *last night* crap again!!!

HARRY. (*Turns, looks at her.*) Why don't you take off that dress and get naked . . . and we'll both walk bare-assed to the end of the pier, and go swimming in the raw 'cause I love ya and I want all my buddies to see it!

GERTRUDE. That's enough!!! (*Furious, she crosses, picks up blanket.*) I'm not stupid!!!! Not one of your dumb waterfront ninnies, who the hell do you think you're talking to!!!! (*Throws blanket behind bar stage right.*)

HARRY. (*Crosses to her.*) You don't understand me! . . . I wanna fix the roof! (*She looks at him, a little dumfounded.*) And paint up this place, 'cause we're staying right here!! (*Looks around the room.*) Yeah! . . . that's right . . . (*Crosses upstage right.*) We're going to make it all festive . . . (*Turns, looks at her.*) With red streamers, 'cause you like red! (*Crosses downstage, looking up at the rafters. He points to them.*) We'll have a row of lanterns over here. And lights hanging down here . . . and all kinds of colored ribbons over here . . . (*Crosses to juke box.*) and there'll be music! And all the guys will be around . . . and they'll be singin 'n' clappin 'n' dancin . . . and you'll be all dressed up in lace! . . . And I'll be behind the bar ya see . . . (*Crosses left, goes behind the bar.*) and I'll be settin up all the drinks . . . and everyone will be toastin! (*He stops, looks at her.*) And if anyone sings that song about you, I'll throw 'em through a wall, 'cause you'll be my wife! (GERTRUDE *stares at him. A beat, then:*) That's right, we're getting married! . . . We're just gonna do it! . . . Ya see, I know what I want, and I don't give a Humping Houdini about nothing else! (*Comes from behind the bar, to* GERTRUDE.) We're going to be so happy, we'll have little Gerties runnin all over the place . . . I got so many plans!

GERTRUDE. (*She crosses downstage right, starts picking up the newspapers.*) Boy . . . you're full of surprises, aren't you?

HARRY. (*Helps her pick up the papers.*) The way I feel inside, we can't miss, you love me and . . .

GERTRUDE. (*Getting angry.*) I don't!!

HARRY. Oh, come on . . . You're so jealous of me all the time and . . .

GERTRUDE. Jealous!!

HARRY. Yeah! . . . Of my babes!

GERTRUDE. I'm not jealous!! I don't want 'em in here, that's all!! . . . It reminds me of the way I used to be . . . no brains and no guts!!! (*She has taken the papers from him, and starts toward the back room.*)

HARRY. (*Crossing after her.*) You're right! I'm tired of laying on all those bones (*She stops near the doorway.*) . . . you'll see, after we're married . . .

GERTRUDE. (*Vehemently throws down the papers, viciously shoves him away from her.*) You simple son of a bitch!!!! . . . I'm setting you straight for the last time!!!! You keep things like they are or get your ass out of here right now!!!!!

HARRY. (*A moment, then:*) . . . Go on with that stuff!

GERTRUDE. Okay . . . (*Goes behind the bar stage right,* HARRY *right behind her.*)

HARRY. You're just upset right now, you'll see that . . . (*She takes a sawed-off baseball bat, turns, faces him. He backs away. She moves toward him, then stops. A moment, then:*) You only use that on bums. (GERTRUDE *doesn't move. Not sure she won't take a swing at him.*) Alright . . .

GERTRUDE. (*A beat, then:*) I won't hear it again? . . . It's over??

HARRY. (*Controlling his own anger.*) Yeah, yeah, yeah, yeah!

GERTRUDE. (*A moment, then, indicating the newspapers near the door.*) Get that mess in back! (*He doesn't respond. She crosses back to the bar, viciously smashes the bat against it.*) I said get it in back!!!! (*He crosses, picks up the papers, starts to exit.*) And I need some booze! (*He stops, looks at her.*) The cheap stuff! A couple of each! (*He exits. She looks after him. Alone now, we see that* GERTRUDE *is wearing down, the confrontations with* HARRY *are beginning to take their toll. She puts the bat away, takes a bottle of vodka off the back shelf, takes a healthy swig. This is the first time we see* GERTRUDE *drink liquor. Periodically, the rattle of bottles has been heard coming from the back room offstage, as* HARRY *selects and puts the liquor in a case.* GERTRUDE *returns the vodka to the shelf. Takes a box of corn flakes and bowl from back counter, pours some flakes, puts the box back. Warms up the coffee.* HARRY *enters, carrying the case of liquor, puts the case on bar, starts crossing to downstage right table.* GERTRUDE *tosses a coin on the bar.*) Let's have a little music! (HARRY *stops, looks at her. A beat, then he continues crossing, sits at table, starts putting on his boots. She crosses to him with corn flakes and spoon, sets them down.*) I made ya some flakes! (HARRY *looks up from lacing his boots. She crosses to downstage center table,*

picks up pitcher of milk and sugar, goes back to him,
puts them down, before she can leave he says:)

HARRY. My dad . . . he loved his flakes. When I was
a kid, he drove a coal truck . . . most of the work was
hand shovelled then, so he used to come home black with
soot . . . (GERTRUDE, *uncomfortable, crosses to down-*
stage center table, picks up oatmeal bowl, coffee cup,
goes behind bar.) you could see these two big white circles
he had for eyes, and all his smiling white teeth. There
were five of us kids, my mom died. One day he said to me
"Son . . . don't ever drive a coal truck" . . . (*Smiles.*)
and he broke up laughing. (GERTRUDE *refills his cup with*
hot coffee, crosses to him.) You'd like my dad, Gert . . .
he's a hell of a guy . . . (*Puts the cup down. Goes be-*
hind the bar. HARRY *continues lacing his boots. A beat,*
then:) What did your husband do? (*She stops what she's*
doing, doesn't move. He looks at her.) I ain't starting
nothing! . . . I just feel like talking, that's all!

GERTRUDE. (*She takes a rag, crosses to downstage*
center table. Wary, not knowing what to make of this.
Not wanting another fight, she gives him the benefit of
the doubt that he only wants to talk. Answers gruffly.)
He was a swab, like you! (*Wipes off the table.*)

HARRY. Oh, yeah? . . . What was his rate?

GERTRUDE. (*Sharply, wanting to end this.*) Bosun!
(*Crosses back behind bar.*)

HARRY. (*Finished lacing his boots.*) Come on over
here, have some coffee with me!

GERTRUDE. (*Her guard still up.*) . . . Yeah . . .
(*Pours herself a cup of coffee.*)

HARRY. (*Pours milk on his flakes.*) He work this port?

GERTRUDE. (*Glares at him.*) I don't want to talk about
it!

HARRY. Oh, ya have to open now, huh?

GERTRUDE. No!

HARRY. Then what's wrong with a little chit-chat. You
know I think one of the guys pointed him out one day,
he lives right around here, doesn't he? (*Starts eating.*)

GERTRUDE. (*Angry.*) No, he doesn't! Look, I don't know what you're doing . . .

HARRY. (*Emphatic, not angry.*) For Christ's sake, I'm just interested, that's all! I mean what's wrong, he's still living, isn't he?

GERTRUDE. Yeah!!

HARRY. Was this his place?

GERTRUDE. No more!!!

HARRY. (*Turns, looks at her.*) A man wants to talk! Nothing else! . . . We got some time before you open, right?

GERTRUDE. Well, change the subject!!

HARRY. (*In disgust as he turns back to the table. Pushes the cereal away.*) . . . Ya got something sweet!?

GERTRUDE. (*Relaxes a little now. Not wanting any more trouble.*) Yeah . . . (*During the following,* GERTRUDE *takes a sweet roll from the cake box, puts it on a plate.*)

HARRY. What about the clothes in my sea bag! . . . can I hang 'em up in the back or something?! My shirt was damp when I put it on this morning!

GERTRUDE. I'll take care of 'em later.

HARRY. I went upstairs, I emptied those pans out . . . you're right, it's a hell of a mess up there! I guess if it ever stops raining, you'll be able to get things dried off and put away . . . I'll give ya a hand!

GERTRUDE. (*With sweet roll and her coffee, she crosses to him.*) I could use it.

HARRY. Yeah, I know ya can! I noticed the toilet was busted!

GERTRUDE. One of those lugs broke it last night. (*Puts down sweet roll. Sips her coffee.*)

HARRY. Alright, I'll tell ya what, after I see Hank about the boat this morning, get that squared away, I'll start working around here, fixing things . . .

GERTRUDE. (*Uncomfortable with his talk about the boat, feeling it might rekindle* HARRY'S *plans again. She sits, says:*) Why don't you forget that boat and work for me, I'll pay ya more than you'd make on that piece of junk! . . . What do ya say?

HARRY. (*A moment, then:*) . . . Why not!

GERTRUDE. All this nonsense is getting us both upset.

HARRY. . . . Yeah, you're right! (*Sips his coffee.*)

GERTRUDE. (*Believing that he's finally getting over all this foolishness, that he's made a concession; she wants to please him.*) And from now on, I bring no one upstairs! . . . But you! (*He looks at her.*) . . . Not that I have since you been staying here. (*A little embarrassed that she revealed this fact, covers it.*) I mean, when ya like playing the tuba . . . you don't trade it in for a flute! (*A beat, then she gets up, standing behind him she starts pulling up his shirt.*) . . . Maybe I'll open late . . . Like you said, we could have all afternoon. What do ya say?

HARRY. (*Wanting much more right now than just going to bed, he gets up, puts coffee cup on table.*) Well, I don't know . . . I mean we're kinda partners now, (*Picks up bowl.*) with me working for ya, all the time, and you paying me a good salary. (*Crosses, goes behind bar.* GERTRUDE *sits back down.*) Well, I gotta help ya more around here then . . . (*Empties cereal into slop bucket, puts bowl into sink. Turns, looks at her.*) and I'll tell ya one thing, you're not going to lose a day of business over me either! (*Seeing she is depressed, a moment, then:*) Hey! (*She turns, looks at him, he smiles.*) . . . We gotta bring in the cheese!

GERTRUDE. Yeah! (*She laughs. Glad to see her happy again he crosses to her, they put their arms around each other.*)

HARRY. They just started cranking chain!

GERTRUDE. What?

HARRY. (*He kneels beside her.*) What's the matter, can't ya hear it? (*She looks at him quizzically. He smiles.*) I'll bet if you closed your eyes you could hear it . . . come on, close your eyes. (*She smiles as he gently touches her face. She closes her eyes, believing things are getting him.* HARRY *softly makes a clanking sound.*) Ya hear it now . . . you see, they're taking up the anchor . . . you can hear the clanking coming from the chain locker . . . oh, she's buried deep, Gert . . . that old chain is strainin' and pulling up a lot of mud . . . we'll be getting under way soon . . . (*Gently, taking her on a sea voyage.*) the engine room gets three bells, (*Sounds three bells.*) all ahead slow . . . you can hear the screw, churning up the water (*Makes sound.*) . . . pushing us out to sea . . .

(GERTRUDE *begins to get involved in spite of herself.* HARRY *gets up now, stands behind her chair, his arms around her, rocks her slowly like the roll of a ship.*) We're out of the breakwater now . . . and you can feel the first roll . . . and you can smell the salt . . . (*Inhales deeply.*) smell it, Gert? . . . Smell that salt? . . . Bridge rings down all ahead half. (*Sounds three bells.*) . . . I'm down in the engine room, see . . . my hands on the throttles . . . I'm watching that PSI gauge holding steady at 450 . . . I get a bell, "Clang-clang." All ahead full! (*Excited now, moves away, spins an imaginary valve.*) I spin the throttle valve open!! I'm losin pressure, I spin 'er back, I yell down to the boiler room . . . (*Stomps his foot on the floor, calls down to boiler room.*) Hey!! "Come on, you guys!!! Main steam pressure is dropping!! Shove in another burner!!!" For Christ sake, tell em Gert, we're losin pressure!!

GERTRUDE. (*Having a great time.*) Come on! come on! ya horse's ass! shove in another burner!!

HARRY. She's coming up now . . . (*To* GERTRUDE.) Watch the gauge, watch the gauge! . . . 430 . . . 440 . . . there she is!! There she is!!! (*Both laugh.*)

GERTRUDE. (*Very excited, gets up.*) What do I do?!? What do I do?!!?

HARRY. (*Moves to her, takes her hand.*) Hell, Gert . . . you're the Captain!! . . . Captain blows the ship's whistle! (*He takes her hand, makes the sound of the ship's whistle, pulling an imaginary rope.*) Come on, do it! (*She joins in, both blowing the whistle. Then he blows the whistle in her face, getting her wet.*)

GERTRUDE. (*She breaks away, laughing.*) I don't want to be the Captain! (*Moves to stage left end of bar, sits.*)

HARRY. (*Laughing, crossing to her.*) Sure ya do!

GERTRUDE. No, I want to be a seaman!!

HARRY. No, you want to be a Captain!!

GERTRUDE. I want to be a *seaman!* I always have, ever since I was a little girl!

HARRY. A seaman?!?

GERTRUDE. I mean it, I really did! My Dad used to bring me down here. (*Gestures toward the front door.*) I used to sit right out there on the pier and watch the ships come in, used to sit for hours, (*He laughs.*) I know it sounds funny, but it got so I could tell 'em all! . . . Almost from the tip of their masts, as they came over the horizon, I could tell ya name, tonnage, and destination . . . I loved my ships . . . and one day, one day, *I* . . . would be a seaman . . . (*A little wistful.*) I didn't know . . . at that age, what do ya know . . .

HARRY. You had it rough, didn't ya?

GERTRUDE. What do you mean?

HARRY. Ah, with your husband.

GERTRUDE. (*She gets up, starts crossing right.*) Let's not start that . . .

HARRY. (*Cutting her off.*) Wait a minute . . . (*Crosses, takes her by the arm.*) We're kind of partners now, see, and no one's gonna hurt you no more!

GERTRUDE. (*Angry, pulls away.*) Don't you worry about that!! Don't you ever worry about that!!!

HARRY. Oh, yeah! Well, I'm tellin ya, if he comes around here, I'll cream him!! (*He crosses, sits at downstage center table.*)

GERTRUDE. (*A beat, then:*) He'd break your skinny back!

HARRY. Oh, yeah?!

GERTRUDE. Yeah!!

HARRY. (*A moment, then, intensely.*) This was *his* place, wasn't it?!

GERTRUDE. (*Furious.*) No, it *wasn't!* Don't you *ever* say that again! This place belonged to my *Dad!* Not to that son of a bitch! . . . He built it when my Mom died!

HARRY. (*A moment, then gently.*) He did one hell of a good job, I'll tell ya that!

GERTRUDE. (*Calmer.*) He did okay . . . with what he had to work with . . . poor guy didn't have much.

HARRY. (*He looks around the bar.*) You must have been a big help to him around here, helping out . . . little added touches . . .

GERTRUDE. No . . . no, I was just a kid when he died, it was left to me in trust . . . Some of his friends boarded it up and it was supposed to be sold . . . anyway, it wasn't. (*From now on,* GERTRUDE *volunteers to talk about her past. Too tired of fending off his questions, she opens up, not aware of his maneuvering to get her to this point.*) Sometime later I got hitched . . . eighteen I was . . . he wasn't bad . . . wasn't a bad man till he got blackballed for drinking on duty. We were married a year at the time . . . he loved his booze . . . it happened more than once, so he got booted out of the union, couldn't ever get another ship . . . after that he changed . . . (*Grins sardonically, gets up, crosses, picks up her coffee cup on upstage right table.*) Yeah . . . he changed . . . one day he opened it up!

HARRY. (*Thinking she is going to continue, then:*) Opened what up?

GERTRUDE. (*A little angry, as she recalls.*) This place! . . . Didn't even ask me, just pulled down the boards and opened 'er up. He had to have work he said . . .

I didn't want to, I begged him! . . . We had to live here, he told me . . . upstairs, it was a storeroom . . . cleaned it out, moved in. I couldn't sleep nights, I remember I used to cry . . . (*Laughs.*) I didn't know any better. He'd come up drunk, three, four in the morning, beat the crap out of me. Then he had me waiting tables . . . you know that was like?!? . . . A young, pretty . . . yeah! . . . I wasn't always fat ya know! . . . I was kind of pretty once!

HARRY. You still are, Gert!

GERTRUDE. (*Angry.*) Oh, bullshit! . . . Feed that crap to someone else, not me, I know what I am! (*Crosses to bar, sits.*)

HARRY. Why did he make you work the place, if you didn't want to!

GERTRUDE. I was good for business! . . . Yeah, real good . . . he left me alone one night . . . I had to close up . . . couple of guys kept hanging around, wouldn't leave . . . they slapped me to the floor and took turns on top of me . . . I think that's funny, don't you? . . . I mean, can you imagine anyone trying that now!

HARRY. (*A beat, then:*) You tell your husband?

GERTRUDE. Yeah . . . he laughed.

HARRY. That bastard! . . . Oh for Christ sake Gert, why the hell didn't ya get out of here then . . .

GERTRUDE. Get out?! . . . Why should I?! (*Goes behind bar. Takes liquor out of case.*) . . . Why should I run, I made it work, *I* made this place pay! He walked out, and I learned! Boy, did I learn! (*Stops what she's doing, glares at him.*) Damn it, you upset me again!! . . . I told you I didn't want to talk about it!!!

HARRY. But we're kinda partners now see . . .

GERTRUDE. (*Realizing that she has been maneuvered into talking about herself.*) Harry, I'm not stupid! I know what you've been doing!

HARRY. Take it easy, baby . . .

GERTRUDE. Don't talk to me like that!!! (*Uncaps the bottles.*)

HARRY. (*Gently.*) What's wrong?

GERTRUDE. You're no different than he was!! . . . Know how to get your way like he did!!! (*During the following, she takes pour spouts out of empty bottles and puts them on the full ones, puts bottles on shelf.*)

HARRY. Come on now . . .

GERTRUDE. You're all bastards! . . . Studs!! . . .

HARRY. (*Angry, gets up, crosses, goes behind bar.*) Hey! Hold on, now!! . . .

GERTRUDE. Without your cock you're useless!! Useless!!! Who needs you!!!!

HARRY. You hold on, damn it!! . . . I'm a man!!! . . . I never hurt no one like that!!!!

GERTRUDE. (*Raging, moving toward him,* HARRY *backing from behind the bar.*) Didn't you!!! . . . I see what ya do to those simple bitches, you wind 'em around your fingers, get 'em to marry ya, then you start using 'em, beating 'em, like he did, he beat me, he beat me bad, look at me!!! . . . Look at me!! I'm a pig!!! I'm a fat pig!!! No one can beat on a fat pig!!!!!

HARRY. I'm not gonna hurt ya! Give me a chance!!

GERTRUDE. (*She goes back, continues putting bottles on shelf.*) No, goddam it, no!!! . . . Who needs you!! . . . Except for a good lay!!!

HARRY. (*He moves to her.*) Hey . . . You was loving me!!

GERTRUDE. No, I wasn't! . . . Damn you, damn you, I wasn't!!!!

HARRY. You was loving me! And you're going to tell me *now!!*

GERTRUDE. (*Shoves him.*) You get away from me!!!

HARRY. You love me! I know it!!

GERTRUDE. (*For the first time, she is frightened of him. She turns, seizes the sawed-off bat,* HARRY *grabs her from behind.*) GET YOUR HANDS OFF ME!!!!

HARRY. (*Furious, pulls her from behind the bar.*) You ain't hitting me with that damn thing!!!! (*In front of bar now.*) Let go!!!!! (GERTRUDE, *struggling desperately*

*to hit him, but his strength is too much for her to cope
with. He finally gets the bat away, throws it upstage
right.*) Take it easy now!! You'll get hurt!!! CALM
DOWN!!!!

GERTRUDE. (*She stops struggling. A moment, then he
lets go her arms. Furious she crosses stage left end of bar.
Viciously slams the top of the bar with her hands.*)
DADDY!!! DADDY!!!

HARRY. He's dead!!!

GERTRUDE. I know!!! (*Shaken by her own behavior,
defends what she has just said.*) I just miss him, that's
all! (*Crosses from behind bar upstage right.*) He used to
sit with me on the pier, when I was real little, talk to
me, tell me stories. "I gotta go now, open up the place,"
he'd say. "You get cold, you call me." He gave me this
big bell, I'd ring it when I wanted him, he'd come running out, with a blanket, my lunch. He used to take my
hand and walk with me, give me pretty colored shells,
he would laugh and skip with me, he loved me.

HARRY. I love you!

GERTRUDE. (*She doesn't respond to him.*) He told me
some day he'd take me out to sea, he would have, I
know.

HARRY. I'll take ya!

GERTRUDE. He was so kind to me, he used to tell me
about my mother, how much she loved me, how pretty she
was. He told me the Sea Horse was a bad place, swearing
'n' drinking, it wasn't good. He said he had to work
here, to have money for us, but he didn't want me
around it, never to come in here he told me, never!
(*Anguished.*) But Frank made me! He made me do it!
I didn't want to!! (*Turns, looks at him, says quietly:*)
He forced me . . . he forced me . . . (*A beat, then, embarrassed, she turns away.*)

HARRY. I know how you feel . . . see something like
that happened to me . . . (*During the following, he goes
behind bar, pours her a cup of coffee. GERTRUDE crosses,
sits stage right end of bar.*) Ya see, when I was a little

guy going to school . . . I was kinda holy, I mean I prayed a lot. I was so religious you know . . . (*Remaining behind bar, he moves to her.*) I remember the Sister took us to our first confession, you know I was scared to death . . . not of the priest . . . I just didn't have anything to confess. So I made up some things, swear words that I never said, said I lied to my dad. Well, I felt so bad later, see, that I lied to a priest, I felt terrible! And then, the Sister said to us, she said that every time you think an evil thought, or do an evil deed . . . a cobweb would form inside ya. Well, I had this crazy imagination, and I know she didn't mean nothing by it . . . but I swear I could feel those cobwebs! I used to forget myself in church and count things instead of paying attention, and think of girls' bottoms and stuff like that. Well, I thought this was a sin, and I was filling my insides with cobwebs . . . it got so bad . . . and one day I got sick . . . oh, I don't know, a bellyache or something, and my Dad came to my room after work, asked me how I was . . . I started crying . . . I told him I was full of webs! (*A beat.*) I told my Dad the whole story then, and he said the Sister didn't mean that as a fact. (*A beat.*) So what I'm saying is . . . I know your Dad told ya the old Horse was a bad place . . . but you just being a little girl 'n' all . . . maybe the same thing happened to you.

GERTRUDE. (*A moment, then, says quietly.*) . . . Maybe . . . maybe.

HARRY. (*Hands her the cup.*) Here . . . have some coffee . . .

GERTRUDE. I don't want any . . . (*She turns away. A beat, then she says simply.*) I was sitting on the pier one day, doing my homework with some friends . . . waiting for my Dad to take me home. I heard all this shouting coming from the Horse. I saw my Dad throw this man out, a couple of other men came out too. This man was trying to hit my Dad . . . I got up and started running towards him . . . crying "Daddy, Daddy!" My Dad

turned to me, and the man stabbed him . . . he died
. . . I held him, and he died. (*She gets up and crosses,
stands near downstage center table. Without emotion
says:*) You know I couldn't remember my name . . .
For the longest time after, I just couldn't think of it,
isn't that strange? . . . Daddy has a sister, so I stayed
with her . . . they had a terrible time with me . . . I
could remember everything that happened that night, all
the questions everyone asked me, I would answer everything right . . . but I couldn't remember my name. My
teacher had to come up and touch me . . . "Gertrude?
Why don't you answer me?" (*A beat, then starts crossing stage left.*) I was okay after awhile . . . finished
school . . . then I started coming down here again, to
watch my ships . . . but I would never go near the
Horse . . . Frank . . . he knew what happened . . .
but thought it was stupid letting this place rot away . . .
When he walked out on me, we owed everyone! I thought
I could make a go of it for awhile . . . *just* . . . to get
things squared away . . . it was bad! (*Sits on bar stool,
left.*) Bums wouldn't pay, just walk out . . . rest of 'em
were no better either, gave me a bad time . . . one day
this swab *grabbed* me . . . I let him have it with a
bottle, right in the face! . . . After that I got respect!
. . . Money! (*Turns, looks at* HARRY.) . . . And I
didn't *need* . . . anyone . . . anymore.

HARRY. (*A moment, then he moves to sea bag, takes
out several shirts, carries bag and shirts to upstage right
table, puts the shirts on a chair. Takes out a large box,
turns, looks at her.*) It's your present! . . . I didn't
leave it aboard, I was mixed up last night! (*He crosses,
hands her the box, she doesn't take it.*)

GERTRUDE. (*Says wearily.*) Not now, okay? . . . I'll
open it later.

HARRY. Ya have to open it now!

GERTRUDE. Please! . . . later, I'll open it later. (*A
moment, then he crosses, box in hand to upstage right
table, as:*)

HARRY. You could never be happy here, Gert . . . so
we'll be leaving . . . No! Not to hide from anyone! . . .
But to start fresh! . . . this is no place to bring up kids!
(*Takes out a penknife, cuts the string on the box.*) I got
a few bucks . . . I can do a lot of things. (*Removing
the cover, puts it on chair.*) I could work that boat, and
make a decent living for us . . . of course I'm not asking
you to go traipsing around with me, until we're married!
(*Folding back the tissue paper, takes out a beautifully
old fashioned wedding dress with a lot of lace.*) Isn't that
somethin'. (*Smoothes it out and crosses to her.*) I think
it's the right size . . . the guy said it was better to have
it a little too big, that way you can always take it in
. . . (*He crosses, stands upstage center, holding the dress
in front of him.*) Now come on, I want ya to be honest
. . . ya don't think it's too fancy, do ya? (*A little uncomfortable now, with* GERTRUDE *just staring at him. He
tries to make light of the situation.*) If you don't like
the color, we could always wash it with my blue socks.
(*No response. Strongly, without anger, says.*) It's a wedding dress! I had it made special, with a lot of lace! I
told the guy to put plenty 'a that on, 'cause you'd like
it! (*Crossing to her, as:*) Ya see . . . I've been plan-
ning this for a long time now . . . (*Lays the dress across
one of the stools.*) and I know I made a lot of mistakes,
I know that . . . but I got the hang of it now . . . ya
see, I want you to marry me, have our kids, and live with
me! (*Quiet determination.*) And you can't tell me you
don't love me . . . no matter what you do, something
tells me you love me . . . it's all over you . . . you
know I can see it in your face right now . . . even your
back says you love me . . . don't ya?

GERTRUDE. (*Moved by his warmth, his sincerity. A
moment, then:*) All the years I've been down here, I
never seen it once . . . where someone wasn't all bullshit
. . . but maybe you changed . . .

HARRY. Oh, I did!

GERTRUDE. (*Gets up, starts crossing upstage left.*) I don't know! . . . *Maybe* you have!

HARRY. Of course I have!!

GERTRUDE. (*Stops. Terribly frustrated, trying not to hurt him, but believing it would never work.*) I'd be too much for you!

HARRY. No, you wouldn't!!

GERTRUDE. Too many things happened!! . . .

HARRY. That stuff doesn't matter to me!!

GERTRUDE. I can't even have kids! (*A moment, then:*) I was hurt once. (*A long pause, then,* HARRY *crosses behind bar. She crosses, sits at downstage center table.*) . . . You don't want someone like me . . . I'm not right for what you want . . . I mean I can get ya laughing, and I know I'm a good bounce . . . but I'm not right for that other . . . family stuff. I like the good times too, and I wouldn't want to change that . . . but you'd never make it with me . . . I'm fat 'n' ugly . . . and it would get to ya . . . in time, it would get to ya . . . you'll make it, but not with me . . . you go.

HARRY. (*A pause, then:*) When I was in Kobe, I saw this little joker hanging around the shipyard . . . just a wee tyke of a guy . . . you know he took to me right off . . . and I know he doesn't have anyone, and you'd like him . . . and if that didn't work out, I'm sure . . . (*He has moved upstage right, turns, looks at her.*) I know it's not gonna be easy, I know that . . . but we can do it! (*Crosses to her.*) And you're not fat! You're well built! And I don't ever want to hear you talking about yourself like that again!

GERTRUDE. The truth is, I don't want what you want anymore.

HARRY. You don't know that!

GERTRUDE. I don't care! . . . Don't you see, I just don't care!

HARRY. Listen, we close up the place for a few weeks, take a little trip somewhere . . . you'll see that . . .

GERTRUDE. (*Gets up.*) No!! . . . I'm not going anywhere with you! Understand?! Nowhere!! (*Crosses to outside door.*)

HARRY. (*Moves after her.*) A couple of days then, all ya need to do is think about it!

GERTRUDE. Now I've got to open up . . . and I want you out of here! (*Unlatches door.*)

HARRY. (*Shocked.*) What?!

GERTRUDE. That's right . . . out!!

HARRY. Why?!?

GERTRUDE. (*A beat.*) Because . . . things are different . . . you changed. (*She goes behind bar stage right.*)

HARRY. (*Realizing she is dead serious and not daring another confrontation, says gently:*) . . . Alright . . . alright . . . we can stay here for a little while then . . . that's fine with me.

GERTRUDE. (*Knowing she must get him out for his own good, that he's just placating her, and will never give up.*) If you forget about getting married!

HARRY. (*Crosses to her behind bar.*) For good? (*No answer.*) . . . Is that what you want? . . . Forget everything? . . . All the plans I been making? . . . Do ya want me to forget everything!?! (*In disgust, he crosses, stands near the jukebox. A beat, then:*) Okay, okay! . . . We forget everything!

GERTRUDE. (*A long pause, then:*) Talker.

HARRY. (*Turns, looks at her.*) What did you say?

GERTRUDE. Talker!

HARRY. (*In disbelief, crossing to her.*) What are you doing to me!

GERTRUDE. Talker!

HARRY. Stop it!!!

GERTRUDE. Talker!

HARRY. You know I ain't talkin! You know I want that kid . . . you know that . . . you know I want that boat!!

GERTRUDE. Talker!

HARRY. (*Explodes.*) Stop it!!!! Alright!!! I'm gonna do it!!!! (*Desperate, as he crosses to his sea bag, stuffs in his shirts.*) I'll show you!!!! I've changed! And if you can't see it you're blind!!!! You watch ol' Harry from now on!!!! You'll see a new man!!!!! You'll see!!!!! (*His sea bag over his shoulder, he goes to outside door.*) YOU'LL SEE ME!!!!!

GERTRUDE. (*She crosses to coat rack, takes his jacket and cap, moves to him. Puts his jacket over his shoulder, hands him his cap.*) You keep warm . . . put on your slicker . . . rain'll get you sick . . . (*She starts crossing to stairwell, stops.*) I tell you what . . . you come back, show me that kid someday and I'll let you come in here. (*He just looks at her, stunned, not knowing what to say or do.*) I'll even break a rule . . . you can bring her in too, if you want. (*A moment, then, sincerely.*) You'll make it, Harry . . . you'll do fine.

HARRY. . . . Upstairs . . . my gear is upstairs.

GERTRUDE. I'll send it on to you later . . . you get settled first. But I'll get your slicker. (*Just before she goes upstairs, turns and looks at him, says:*) Don't forget that dress. (*Exits. A moment, then he angrily puts down the sea bag, puts on his jacket as he crosses to wedding dress, picks it up and crosses back. Not wanting to stuff the dress into the bag, he hesitates, disgusted, he throws it on one of the chairs, puts on his cap. GERTRUDE enters carrying his slicker, crosses, hands it to him. He pulls it out of her hands, stuffs it into his bag. He ties his bag as GERTRUDE goes behind the bar, puts on her apron. He zips up his jacket.*) Just leave the door open . . . they'll be coming in now. (HARRY *watches* GERTRUDE *as she takes the coin she had put on the bar, crosses to the juke box, inserts it, and makes a selection. A moment, then the record* Plucking the Blues, *a rock and roll number, comes on at low volume. She goes back behind the bar.* HARRY *puts his sea bag over his shoulder, crosses to front door, stops a few moments, then he turns, says:*)

HARRY. I ain't going! . . . (*He crosses to bar.*) You hear me?! . . . I said I ain't going!! (GERTRUDE *crosses* to juke box.) . . . 'cause you need me!! (*She turns the volume up full, the music is deafening.* HARRY *throws down his sea bag.*) No I ain't going!! You hear me!! (*Takes off his cap and jacket, throws them down violently.*) YOU'RE GONNA MARRY ME!!! (*Crosses right up to her.*) YOU'RE GONNA MARRY ME!!!! (*He goes to juke box, yanks out the plug. There is a dead silence. She says quietly:*)

GERTRUDE. . . . I don't trust you . . .

HARRY. (*He crosses slowly toward her.*) You will . . .

GERTRUDE. I don't trust you . . . I don't trust you . . . (*Moving close to her,* GERTRUDE *backing away.*) I don't trust you, I don't trust you . . . (*He gently takes her arms, drawing her close to him.*) I don't trust you . . . (*She's in his arms now.*)

HARRY. You will . . . I know you will!

THE END

PROPERTY PLOT

Top of Show Set-up:

Front Door Outside:
    sign reading "Sea Horse Bar"
    hanging light above sign (lit)
    heavy bolt inside of door

Inside Barroom:
    3 tables
    hanging light above each table (lit)
    6 chairs
    portable stove
    bar
    4 bar stools
    bulletin board with postcards, notices, personal ads, photos
        and special notice
    coat tree with several empty hangers and leis
    5 coat hooks on upstage right wall (empty)
    juke box with teddy bear, giraffe and small monkey on top
    fold-out postcards on walls next to juke box
    practical neon Ballantine Ale sign above juke box (lit)
    Heineken Beer plaque next to juke box
    photos of ships
    small calendar, shells, several starfish fastened to wall

Above Bar:
    2 fluorescent lights (lit)

On Top of Bar:
    salt, pepper, Tabasco sauce, napkin holder (For personal use,
        does not serve food)
    6 dirty beer mugs
    5 coasters
    swizzle sticks
    5 ashtrays
    2 damp rags
    1 shot glass
    2 dirty coffee mugs
    1 tray with damp rag
    bowl with candy
    pack of cigarettes with matches

Under Bar:
  water in plastic dishpan used as sink
  3 clean glasses
  slop bucket
  canvas money bag
  apron
  2 pencils
  ledger book
  sawed-off baseball bat hanging on nail
  1 box kitchen matches
  box of cornflakes
  cookie tin
  cup with coins for juke box
  1 box raisins

Behind Bar:
  First shelf:
    cash register with 2 packets of real money with play money
        for fill, plus $19.00 in singles
    mirror
    liquor bottles with pour spouts
    4 empty liquor bottles with pour spouts
  Second shelf:
    glasses
    beer mugs
  Third shelf:
    glasses
    liquor bottles
    sea shells
  Fourth shelf:
    liquor bottles
  4 ft. orange ladder with towels on rungs
  trash bucket
  table with slop pan

Small Refrigerator:
  soft drink bottles inside, filled with water
  pitcher of milk inside

Counter with double hot plate:
  large enamel coffee pot (3 qt.)

Second Counter:
 Top:
  small 2 burner hot plate
  2 glass coffee pots
  bread box with sweet roll
  sugar bowl
 Bottom shelf:
  faded blue towel, plates
 Second shelf:
  saucers, bowls, coffee cups, box of cookies
 Top drawer:
  knives, forks, spoons
 hanging light in hall leading upstairs

Act Two:
 spread newspapers (used as mattress)
 blanket on top of newspapers
 sea bag (used as pillow)
 place duplicate dry jacket on coat tree
 place duplicate dry jeep cap on coat tree
 strike wet jacket, jeep cap, sweat shirt
 place duplicate dry boots near D. S. R. table
 place pot of oatmeal on hot plate—turn on switch
 wooden spoon on plate near oatmeal
 dishrag near oatmeal
 oatmeal box on table
 fresh coffee on small hot plate—perking
 wipe up soda (water) Gertrude threw in Harry's face

Off-stage Right:
 bottles in box for sound effect
 mop and bucket of water
 cleaning rag
 blanket
 stack of L.A. newspapers
 old pot with oatmeal and wooden spoon
 oatmeal box
 liquor case with full bottles
 duplicate dry jacket
 duplicate dry jeep cap
 duplicate dry boots

Off-stage Left:
  portable phonograph
  record
  black slicker
  bucket of water

PERSONAL PROPS

Harry:
  1 cigar in plastic wrapper (put in jacket pocket after wetting
      down)
  sea bag (21″ x 34″) containing:
    wedding dress box (19½″ x 12½″ x 3½″, ¼″ plywood
        reinforced)
  old fashioned wedding dress in box tied with string
  foam padding packed around box to give bulk without extra
      weight
  6 shirts packed on top of box
  small pocket knife on leather strap hooked on belt

Gertrude:
  1 hair band on wrist

COSTUME PLOT

Act One:

GERTRUDE:
   dark green men's work pants
   long-sleeved grey men's work shirt
   black shoes
   men's tie used as belt
   blue bandana for her hair

HARRY:
   light-weight blue jacket
   dark green sweat shirt
   tan gabardine pants
   black leather belt
   logger's low-top lace boots
   knee pads
   sweat socks
   Army jeep cap
   handkerchief

Act Two:

GERTRUDE:
   blue and red flowered dress with red crepe flower at neckline
   tan sandals

HARRY:
   black and red plaid shirt
   duplicate gabardine tan pants
   black leather belt
   white sweat socks

Pre-set:
   duplicate jacket
   duplicate boots
   duplicate jeep cap

MUSIC

Prelude to Act One and Act Two:
RCA LSP-4135 "Lovers Guitar" Chet Atkins
"La Madrugada" (The Early Dawn)

Act One: Gertrude's Dance
RCA LSP-4135 "Lovers Guitar" Chet Atkins
"Cajita de Musica" (Little Music Box)
(splicing to elongate necessary)

Act Two: Juke box
Enjoy Records—45 RPM
ZTSP 98719
"Picking the Blues"
Elmore James 2015

NOTE: Not public domain

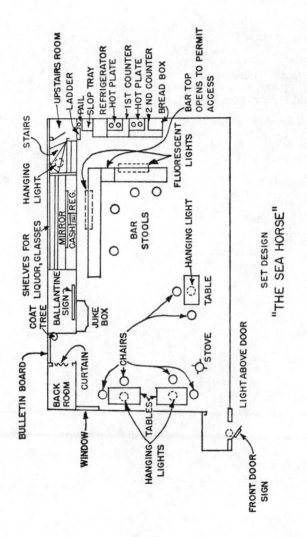

SET DESIGN
"THE SEA HORSE"

64

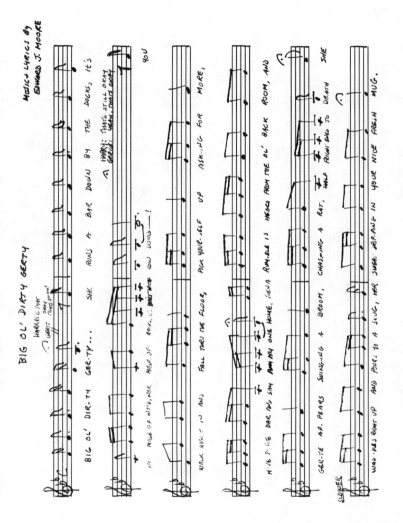

BIG OL' DIRTY GERTY

MUSIC & LYRICS BY
EDWARD J. MOORE

HOME-BUILT

Lighting Equipment

for The Small Stage

By THEODORE FUCHS

This volume presents a series of fourteen simplified designs
for building various types of stage lighting and control equip-
ment, with but one purpose in mind—to enable the amateur
producer to acquire a complete set of stage lighting equip-
ment at the lowest possible cost. The volume is 8½" x 11" in
size, with heavy paper and spiral binding—features which
make the volume well suited to practical workshop use.

Community Theatre

A MANUAL FOR SUCCESS

By JOHN WRAY YOUNG

The ideal text for anyone interested in participating in Community Theatre as a vocation or avocation. "Organizing a
Community Theatre," "A Flight Plan for the Early Years,"
"Programming for People—Not Computers," and other chap-
ters are blueprints for solid growth. "Technical, Business and
Legal Procedures" cuts a safe and solvent path through some
tricky undergrowth. Essential to the library of all community
theatres, and to the schools who will supply them with talent
in the years to come.

The Happy Hunter

(ALL GROUPS)
Comedy—CHARLES FEYDEAU

English Adaptation by Barnett Shaw
7 Men, 3 Women—2 Interiors

Chandel tells Yvonne he is going hunting with Castillo, but when Castillo turns up unexpectedly, she sees the hoax, and therefore decides to yield to Roussel's amorous advances, going to his bachelor den with him. But, across the hall, Chandel is having a rendezvous with Madame Castillo. A hectic evening ensues, complicated by an eccentric landlady and by the appearance of Yvonne's nephew, whose girl friend used to live there. The police, seeking Madame Castillo's lover, grab Roussel, while Chandel escapes through the window and runs off with Roussel's trousers. The mix-up unravels in act three, with one surprise after the other, Yvonne winning all tricks while her husband gets the punishment.

ROYALTY, $35-$25

A Gown for His Mistress

(Little Theatre) Farce
GEORGE FEYDEAU

English Translation by Barnett Shaw
4 Men, 6 Females—Interior
Can be played 1900 Period or Chic Modern

A wild and saucy matrimonial mix-up by the celebrated author of A FLEA IN HER EAR.

Dr. Moulineaux stays out all night after a futile attempt to meet his mistress, Suzanne, at the Opera Ball. He tells his wife he has been up all night with a friend, Bassinet, who is near death, but at that moment Bassinet walks in. Upbraided by his mother-in-law for his infidelity, he decides he must no longer allow Suzanne to pretend to be a patient. For a hide-away, he rents an apartment that formerly belonged to a dressmaker. In Act II he is courting Suzanne in his new apartment when her husband walks in. Posing as a dressmaker he gets rid of the husband momentarily, but is caught in a desperate entanglement when his wife, his mother-in-law, Bassinet, and Bassinet's wife appear. In Act III, Moulineaux's household is in an uproar but he manages to lie his way out of it all with the help of Bassinet who has a photograph that seems to solve everything. Outstanding male and female roles. The play moves rapidly and is an excellent work-out for alert actors and actresses.

ROYALTY, $35-$25

HANDBOOK

for

THEATRICAL APPRENTICES

By Dorothy Lee Tompkins

Here is a common sense book on theatre, fittingly sub-titled, "A Practical Guide in All Phases of Theatre." Miss Tompkins has wisely left art to the artists and written a book which deals only with the practical side of the theatre. All the jobs of the theatre are categorized, from the star to the person who sells soft drinks at intermission. Each job is defined, and its basic responsibilities given in detail. An invaluable manual for every theatre group in explaining to novices the duties of apprenticeship, and in reassessing its own organizational structure and functions.

"If you are an apprentice or are just aspiring in any capacity, then you'll want to read and own Dorothy Lee Tompkins' A HANDBOOK FOR THEATRICAL APPRENTICES. It should be required reading for any drama student anywhere and is a natural for the amateur in any phase of the theatre."—George Freedley, Morning Telegraph.

"It would be helpful if the HANDBOOK FOR THEATRICAL APPRENTICES were in school or theatrical library to be used during each production as a guide to all participants."—Florence E. Hill, Dramatics Magazine.

Going Ape

NICK HALL

(Little Theatre.) Farce.
3 male, 2 female—Interior

This hilarious and almost indescribable farce has some serious undertones. Rupert, an idealistic and romantic young orphan, has come to his uncle's house to commit suicide. This proves to be no easy matter. For one thing he is constantly attended by his uncle's attractive nurse/secretary. He is also constantly interrupted by a stream of visitors, at first fairly normal, but increasingly incredible. Rupert realizes that all the visitors are the same three people, and his attention is drawn toward understanding the preposterously Victorian plot in which he is trapped, and which, in a startlingly theatrical climax, he begins to understand. "An intricate plot with subtle foreshadowing and a grab bag of surprises . . . some of the funniest characters you'll ever see molded into a tight dramatic package."— News, Fort Myers. "Every scene transcends not only the imagination, but melds into a literally death-defying whole. It's fast, like 2,000 mph . . . a play as old and as contemporary as today." Sarasota Journal. "Going Ape is truly zany . . . the wackiness is infectious." —Time.

(Royalty, $50-$25.)

Eat Your Heart Out

NICK HALL

(Little Theatre.) Comedy.
3 male, 2 female—Interior

In this theatrical comedy Charlie, an out of work actor currently employed as a waiter, takes the audience through a sequence of hilarious encounters in a succession of Manhattan restaurants. By changing the tablecloths during the course of the action the basic setting of three tables and six chairs becomes a variety of New York restaurants, both elegant and shabby. The scenes change, the action is uninterrupted and the comedy never stops. The other performers play several parts: the girl desperately trying to eat snails and oysters to please her fiance; the middle-aged couple whose marriage is breaking up; the lovers so intent on each other they cannot order dinner; the rich, embittered astrologer; the timid man who never gets a waiter; the agents, directors, actors, and waiters. An amusing gallery of characters whose stories intertwine and finally involve Charlie. The author of "Accommodations" has written a very funny, contemporary play that is also a serious comedy of backstage life. ". . . a sharp, stunning play. It'll make you howl—but better yet, it might even make you sniffle a bit."—Fort Lauderdale News. "Tightly written and very, very entertaining. I recommend it enthusiastically."—Miami Herald. ". . . About as good as anything I've ever seen in dinner theater . . ."—Fort Lauderdale Times.

(Royalty, $50-$25.)

THE LADY WHO CRIED FOX!!!

(LITTLE THEATRE—COMEDY)

By EDWARD CLINTON

3 men, 2 women—Interior

When a jealous actor who's always on the road, finds out his wife has taken on a young male roommate to meet expenses, the show does not go on. He immediately returns home to find out what's going on. The roommate, an inventor who likes to roller skate, is caught in the middle between a jealous husband and frustrated wife. Eventually, all five of the characters get into the act and the result is just plain fun. ". . . punch and humor . . . a funny play. . . ." — Miami Herald. ". . . clever script . . . intriguing sense of humor coupled with a powerful knack for drama. . . ." —Fort Lauderdale News. ". . . funny, delightful and above all devoid of the off color material so many writers feel is essential. . . ." —Hollywood, Fla. Sun Tattler.

(Royalty, $50-$35.)

NOT WITH MY DAUGHTER

(LITTLE THEATRE—COMEDY)

By JAY CHRISTOPHER

3 men, 3 women—Interior

Will Gray suddenly has a problem. His 18-year-old daughter appears at his "swinging singles" apartment door. It seems Will and his neighbor, Rip Tracy, a velvet-voiced radio Dee Jay have a penchant for juggling girls like antacid tablets. Poor Will has a go-go girl in the living room—with her motor running—and a devoted young lady in the bedroom—but that's o.k. since she loves him. Rip has a girl in his apartment already when Will calls on him to also entertain the go-go girl. Then Will's daughter appears to complicate matters further—not only are explanations in order—but daughter has problems of her own. How it all is resolved will leave the audience limp with laughter. An adult play with not one leering joke. It's all in fun. "Funny? Absolutely." —High Point, N.C. Enterprise. ". . . a laugh riot . . ." —Greensboro, N.C. Daily News. ". . . fast-paced farce with as many laughs as you can handle in one sitting." —Lexington, Ky. Herald.

(Royalty, $50-$25.)

HERE'S HOW

A Basic Stagecraft Book

THOROUGHLY REVISED
AND ENLARGED

by HERBERT V. HAKE

COVERING 59 topics on the essentials of stagecraft
(13 of them brand new). *Here's How* meets a very
real need in the educational theater. It gives to directors and others concerned with the technical
aspects of play production a complete and graphic
explanation of ways of handling fundamental stagecraft problems.

The book is exceptional on several counts. It not only
treats every topic thoroughly, but does so in an easy-
to-read style every layman can understand. Most important, it is prepared in such a way that for every
topic there is a facing page of illustrations (original
drawings and photographs)—thus giving the reader a
complete graphic presentation of the topic along with
the textual description of the topic.

Because of the large type, the large size of the pages
(9" x 12"), and the flexible metal binding, *Here's
How* will lie flat when opened and can be laid on a
workbench for a director to read while in a *standing*
position.